# Theology

AN ASSESSMENT OF CURRENT TRENDS

## STAFF OF THE LUTHERAN CHURCH IN AMERICA
## TASK GROUP FOR LONG-RANGE PLANNING

| | | |
|---|---|---|
| Harold E. Berg | Commission on Church Papers | 1/1/66-3/31/68 |
| Dana H. Johnson | Commission on Evangelism | 1/1/66-3/31/68 |
| Lois I. Leffler | Lutheran Church Women | 1/1/66-3/31/68 |
| Luther R. Livingston | Commission on Stewardship | 1/1/66-6/30/66 |
| John M. Mangum | Board of World Missions | 1/1/66-7/31/67 |
| Beryl B. Maurer | Board of American Missions | 1/1/66-6/30/67 |
| Lawrence E. Nelson | Commission on Youth Activities | 11/1/66-1/31/67 |
| Richard J. Niebanck | Board of Social Ministry | 1/1/66-3/31/68 |
| Marcus F. Otterbein | Board of Parish Education | 1/1/66-3/31/68 |
| Donald R. Pichaske | Board of Parish Education | 1/1/66-3/31/68 |
| Franklin H. Schott | Board of American Missions | 7/1/67-2/29/68 |
| Mrs. John P. Shannon | Commission on Youth Activities | 10/1/67-1/31/68 |
| Leonard A. Sibley | Board of Parish Education | 1/1/66-3/31/68 |
| Wilbur G. Volker | Board of Parish Education | 1/1/66-3/31/68 |
| William E. Wendt | Board of Parish Education | 1/1/66-5/20/66 |
| John J. Ziegler, Jr. | Commission on Youth Activities | 1/1/66-10/31/66 |
| | Edward W. Uthe, Director | |

# THEOLOGY
## AN ASSESSMENT OF
## CURRENT TRENDS

REPORT OF THE LUTHERAN CHURCH IN AMERICA

TASK GROUP FOR LONG-RANGE PLANNING

**EDWARD W. UTHE,** Director

FORTRESS PRESS               PHILADELPHIA

© 1968

BOARD OF PUBLICATION

OF THE

LUTHERAN CHURCH IN AMERICA


Library of Congress Catalog Card Number 68-55757


355G68     Printed in U.S.A.     1-1016


Scripture quotations from the *Revised Standard Version of the Bible*, copyrighted 1946 and 1952 by the Division of Christian Education, National Council of Churches, are used by permission.

# CONTENTS

# Preface

In an attempt to prepare for the decade from 1970 to 1980 the Lutheran Church in America created a Task Group for Long-Range Planning to conduct a planning study. The task group was given the assignment of forecasting the shape of the society in which and to which the church will be ministering, assessing trends in theological thought, interpreting trends in the life and work of the church, and, finally, suggesting the major issues with which the Lutheran Church in America should be concerned in the 1970's. Findings of the task group are intended to be used primarily by LCA boards and commissions as a guide to policy formulation and program development for the next decade.

A small mountain of working papers was produced by the task group. The ore has been mined and refined. It now exists chiefly in the form of a task-group report *Significant Issues for the 1970's* and in supporting documents such as the one you are now reading. From the inception of the project it was felt that the theological disciplines are important sources of the church's conception of itself and its relationship to society. Theology provides norms and goals for the nature and mission of the church. It is a necessary foundation for action on the part of the church. The function of the present document is to identify major trends in current theological thought as they occur in doctrinal formulations, biblical interpretation, analyses of Christian ethics, viewpoints on ecumenism, history, tradition, and reflection on the church and its mission. Material which contributed to the development of the task-group report is here made available to supplement the report.

Three questions guided the task-group study of trends in theology. The present document addresses itself chiefly to the first two. It provides a preliminary consideration of the third question, which is dealt with in more detail in the task-group report *Significant Issues for the 1970's*. The three questions are:

1. What are the directions in which current theological thought appears to be moving?

2. What are the key theological issues which persons are likely to face during the next ten years?

3. How can the church assist persons to deal with these issues in ways which are meaningful and relevant?

This report on current trends in theology is the end product of an extensive study of the field by task-group members. Thirty-four theologians, biblical scholars, and church leaders were interviewed at the outset to determine the major dimensions involved in a study of current theological trends. This was followed by library research by task-group members, preparation of working papers on particular topics, and preparation of a review draft of this report on theological trends. The review draft was evaluated by fifteen theological school professors during a two-day consultation. Subsequently, the report was revised on the basis of suggestions made at the consultation and was prepared in its present form.

Theology is a basic constituent of self-awareness on the part of Christians and the church. It contributes to the formation and preservation of a sense of Christian identity. The survival of any personal or social entity requires formation and preservation of the inner identity which constitutes it and guarantees its continuance as a unique entity. For a social entity this function is performed by collective remembering and is incorporated in tradition. Collective remembering includes what is written. More importantly, it consists of the internalization of the tradition by each member of the community—a process by which each person in the community adopts its past as his own and is thereby changed in his present existence. Each person participates in a common memory and a common hope. One task of theology is to give articulate expression to the church's collective remembering and reflecting upon its origin, its message, and its mission. In order to contribute to the development of a contemporary Christian identity, theology must speak in formulations that are intellectually comprehensible to modern man, and which at the same time communicate with the deep religious needs of humanity. The pages that follow describe theology's current attempts to do so.

# I

# Theological Responses to the Present Challenge

## I. THE CONTEXT AND EMPHASES OF CONTEMPORARY THEOLOGY

Christian theology seeks to spell out the meaning of God in relation to man, history, and the world, and the meaning of man, history, and the world in relation to God. Most of the church's theology, especially that theology generally considered as "great" or "epoch-making," is far from being a private monologue carried on inside an ivory tower. It is a living dialogue with the world and history. From Paul to Luther, from Augustine to Reinhold Niebuhr, from Origen to Tillich, Christian theology has, at its best, been carried on in dialogue with the world. Whether irenic or polemic, whether critical or appreciative, the church's word concerning the world is inseparable from her word about herself and about God.

Theology is by nature a reflective activity. It is reflective in a double sense. Actively, theology reflects *upon*. Passively, it is a reflection *of*. In the active sense, theology is the disciplined reflection by the believing community *upon* the revelation that has been entrusted to it. The primary datum of such reflection is the biblical witness of ancient Israel and of the primitive church to the revelation of God in and through history. The other data of theological reflection include the accumulation of past reflection (theology is an ongoing "reflection upon reflection") as well as the traditions of cultus and preaching which lie at the heart of the church's life. Finally, theology reflects upon the challenges of contemporary history and, out of the depth of its own life, seeks to speak a meaningful word of interpretation.

Theology is always the reflection *of* particular historical circumstances. To a large extent secular history writes the agenda for theology. Whether the circumstances be the fall of the Roman Empire, the rise of Nazism, or the technological revolution, theology is to some degree a response to the anxiety or optimism that dominates a particular period. It is precisely because of the continually changing agenda which history presents to theology that the church's cumulative reflection is so rich and varied. As with the "primitive" theologies of the biblical writers, so with the theologians of succeeding ages: in its language, form, and emphasis, theology is the reflection of the church's historical *Sitz im Leben*.

In doing theology the church engages in dialogue with its own peculiar past and with the contemporary world. This dialogue is of a double character: *internal* among the variety of traditions and contemporary approaches within the believing community, and *external* with the larger community of men in terms of history's agenda.

Faithfulness to the essentially historical character of revelation requires Christian theology to acknowledge with candor that its discourse is shaped by historical forces. Beginning with the biblical assertion that God is active in history, and appropriating anew the self-correcting variety of reflections by past generations of believers, theology can and must welcome the opportunity to reconstruct itself in the light of both current developments and its own special history.

It is generally recognized that the present is an age of sharply accelerating change. The most descriptive term applicable to the dramatic increases in such disparate phenomena as growth of population and of knowledge are the terms "explosion" and "avalanche." The rapidity of technological and social change seems currently to produce a line curving steeply upward. Momentous changes are forcing man to drastically alter his way of thinking about himself and his world. Earlier spatial models which men used to understand reality are giving way to temporal, dynamic, or relational models. The world is no longer thought of as a place where change occurs; rather, the world is change itself. It is in the continuous process of developing.

The challenge and demand presented by this situation are unprecedented. Rapid change will most likely be the order of the day for the immediate future, with continued acceleration of technology, knowledge, government operation, and production. Consolidation of gains cannot be counted on to take place leisurely in "plateau" periods. The social organism's task of catching up with and integrating scientific and technological advances will have to be pursued even as science and technology leapfrog ahead to render nascent consolidations obsolete before they are complete.

This situation of rapid and critical change on many fronts has a profound effect on the theological enterprise. Critical upheavals of past history were occasions which brought forth monuments of theological system-building: Augustine's *City of God*, Calvin's *Institutes*, or Barth's *Church Dogmatics*. The reverse seems to be occurring today. Theological architectonics seems to be as much a thing of the past as substance philosophy and spatial models. System-building takes too long. A full-blown theological system is likely to be obsolescent before it is completed. For many, methodology, the devising of methods of theological investigation, has replaced system-building. Others confine their investigations to narrowly defined subjects: religious language, the "empirical" church, hermeneutical problems, to name but a few. For the present, theologians seem content to dwell in intellectual tents and prefabs. Should theological edifices ever be constructed again, they will doubtless be radically different from earlier structures. Movement, relation, and a tentative open-endedness will replace the completeness, symmetry, and finality of earlier efforts.

The present period is marked by what may be described as the final phase in the process of secularization which began as long ago as the Renaissance. The long-established distinction between the natural and the supernatural seems to have broken down. Today man has to discover anew the meaning of "natural." Old distinctions are meaningless. Authority is no longer "from above," either in the church or in secular life. In the latter it emerges in clearly political terms amid the contending and countervailing powers that make up society. In the former it comes forth from the living dialogue which takes place within the believing community as it confronts the world.

In both the developing and the technologically advanced nations of the world, human destiny is seen in almost completely social and political terms. While the perils of technology, weapons technology especially, may provoke second thoughts in some otherwise optimistic observers, it is hard to resist the conclusion that men are in increasing numbers becoming enthralled by visions of unlimited human possibilities. For these men, engrossed in the functional and pragmatic, such transcendent categories as "God" seem to have no meaning whatever. In such a context, God-talk seems to some theologians to be, for the present, totally impossible. The radical "death of God" theologians, largely of a Barthian lineage, are the most publicized of those theologians reflecting this sense of futility. The chief contribution of these "radicals" is that they are vivid symptoms of an age in which there has been a serious breakdown of God-language as any sort of meaningful discourse for vast numbers of contemporary men.

Secularization has produced a trend that affects theology generally: a growing interest in subject matter not traditionally associated with theological investigation, subject matter decidedly this-worldly and nonecclesiastical—in a word, secular. It is the conviction of many theologians that clues to ultimate meaning are to be discovered through encounter and dialogue with such subjects as natural science, politics, and sociology. Underlying is the assumption that the God whose self-revelation is attested to in the Bible is now present amid the changes and conflicts of present history. To discern God's presence, therefore, it seems as necessary to be involved in what is going on in the contemporary world as it is necessary to have a grounding in the traditions of the believing fellowship. The latter requirement cannot be bypassed, as many observers fear it may be, amid current interest in the secular. Being *in* the world is necessary, but no meaningful interpretation *of* the world can be made without the perspective which is afforded by the confrontation with divine revelation within the believing fellowship.

Along with rapid change and secularization, the communications revolution is a third characteristic of the present period. Growth of the means of human communication has been so fast that it is no longer possible for any person or community to live in isolation. For theology this means that particular theological traditions can no longer operate in separate compartments. Dialogue across the lines of confession will increase. While different traditions will continue to be discernible, theologians associated with them will have the benefit of correctives and qualifiers which dialogue affords. Theology will become increasingly ecumenical. The theological enterprise can no longer be carried on in relative isolation from the world. Events of contemporary history will more and more require theologians to test the validity of their assertions, not only against the past witness of the believing community, but also against the demands and challenges of the world. Dialogue with the secular disciplines will continue to grow.

The explosive changes of the present have tended to shatter the patterns in which man has traditionally found meaning and direction for his life, both individual and corporate. We live in a time when forms in which the Christian message has traditionally been presented have lost meaning for major segments of the population. Crucial concerns are concepts of man and of God. For much of contemporary culture the word "God" has become an empty sound. This is a problem not only for Christians trying to communicate with the intelligentsia, but also for the urban or suburban pastor as he deals with his most sensitive church leaders and youth.

Dialogue with the contemporary world has forced theology to make a radical reappraisal of its tools and methods. Even in the absence of widespread attempts at system-building, a number of careful efforts are being made to relate Christian thought to various contemporary frames of reference. Although these approaches differ quite widely from each other, certain common themes or concerns run through all of them. Before looking at the responses of specific theologians and theological schools, we shall attempt to sketch two of these overarching themes: a growing sense of the importance of "the secular" and a growing awareness of the importance of history.

## The Importance of the Secular

However varied the starting-points and methods of contemporary theology, one element cuts across all of them: a sharp interest in "the secular." By secular is meant the empirical world of time and space—all of material, organic, social, and historical existence. This concern stems from a variety of roots: Barth's distinction between Christian faith and religion; Bonhoeffer's comments on "worldly Christianity"; reaction against an over-concern for personal salvation and corresponding works of piety to develop the "inner life" of the believer; dissatisfaction with the self-concern of the institutional church and its loss of sense of mission and service to the world. Theologians are insisting that we must take seriously all of the world, since all of existence is subject to God's lordship and is the arena of his activity.

Growing recognition of the importance of the secular has influenced the ways in which theologians go about their work. The most distinctive new element is the so-called theology of engagement. This refers to the conscious theological reflection being done by Christians as they actively confront and seek to bear a valid witness in new secular situations—the urban slums, government and politics, the intellectual and artistic communities. These theologians feel that meaningful theological approaches cannot be developed in isolation from the world. They begin with the analogy popularized by Harvey Cox of God's work as a floating crap game and the church as a confirmed gambler eager each day to find out where the action is. They plunge into the involvement of the life of the world, not knowing what will happen, but asking with an urgency that is definitely not academic: "What does it mean to be the people of God in these circumstances? What form must our life take to be faithful and valid? What do these experiences tell us about the nature and activity of God?" They take the position that the good for which Christians and non-Christians strive cannot be defined in terms of principles and precepts. It is a question of relationships and acts pointing to opportunities for human fulfillment—opportunities which God opens up at a particular time and place on the road to the future. Guidance cannot be provided primarily by any systematic rational set of values, but rather by participation in the koinonia where God's work becomes visible through word, sacrament, and interrelatedness.

Theologians of engagement use the tools provided by academic disciplines, but think in forms that are open-ended and organic in character. They tend to be less interested in metaphysics (even if they are philosophically sophisticated), much less interested in discovering underlying structures of a natural law character. Some of these theologians have completely dismissed all traditional theology and philosophy as irrelevant and are in danger of being swallowed up by their zeal for relevance. Their loss of historic rootage in the intellectual Christian tradition makes it difficult for them to do more than reflect contemporary society in the passive sense and leaves no room for the critical "reflecting upon" which is also an essential element in theology.

Like the theologians of engagement, academic theologians have also been influenced by the emerging concern for the secular. They feel, however, that some sort of theological synthesis is not only a possibility but also a most urgent necessity. They do not minimize the breakdown of the former ethos and the unsuitability of its language and thought forms, but they contend that an intensification of systematic theological effort is called for, making use of such tools as metaphysics, natural science, and historical criticism. They tend to begin their thinking in terms of a secular discipline, seeking to use the secular discipline as a meaningful vehicle for the contemporary expression of Christian theology. The rationale for this approach is that the history of Christian theology gives reason to believe that there are many philosophies, epistemologies, anthropologies, which can furnish a framework for a theology by which the meaning of the Christian scripture can be stated. The ongoing work of the Spirit in the history of the church gives us the right to attempt contemporary statements.

The engagement and academic approaches are related. Theologians of engagement proceed in a less neatly defined fashion, dealing with existence on an ad hoc basis in contrast to the more systematic approach of the academic theologian. But the "engagement" men owe their basic orientation to the academics (many of them to the post-Barthians); and the academics show an increased interest in subjects which have long been the concern of the men engaged on the firing line of politics, economics, and civil rights.

Theological formulations about the nature of this world and its relationship to God differ sharply. On the one hand are theologians who may be categorized as "quasi-sacramentalists" or "immanentists." These theologians try to identify the presence and activity of God in the dynamic process of this-worldly existence. They tend to avoid the sharp distinction between nature and grace which characterized the Reformation theology. Redemption is seen as involving the entire process of the world's history and evolution, rather than the individual's personal relationship to God. The immanentist view of the world is held by such widely disparate schools as those of Tillich (self-transcending or belief-ful realism), Chardin (the presence of Omega-Christ in evolving reality) and process theology (where the being of God, if not actually identified with the evolution of reality, is intimately involved with it).

These theologians can also be called translators, because they tend to feel that the most pressing theological task today is the cogent restatement of the fact that divine grace permeates the creation and that this restatement must be both faithful to the intention of the historic Christian tradition and intelligible within the genuinely new contemporary situation. It is within the context of this approach that we find a great interest in interdisciplinary dialogue between theology and the natural sciences (e.g., Philip J. Hefner) and between theology and the arts (e.g., Joseph Sittler).

In contrast to the theologians described above stand those who style themselves "radicals" in the sense of seeking to get back to the essential roots of Christianity. They may also be described as "transformers." They feel that the theological structure of traditional Christianity is meaningless in our present situation and must be radically transformed. They tend to reduce theology to Christology and, in some cases, to reduce Christology to ethics. This movement has a sociological orientation and includes such diverse elements as Cox's earlier uncritical celebration of the "secular city," various critiques of the empirical church, and Hamilton's assertion that man come-of-age is prepared to meet and handle his own problems without divine assistance.

Langdon Gilkey has identified the distinctive roots and features of this movement. The movement has accepted Barth's radical separation of the sacred and the secular, of God and ordinary experience, of theology and philosophy. It approves his separation of Christianity and religion and the centering of theological and religious concerns solely in Jesus Christ. It has accepted Tillich's campaign against theism and against personalist and mythological language about God. It has absorbed

Bultmann's argument against "mythological" categories in theology, both in biblical-kerygmatic language and in objective theological language about God. It agrees with Bultmann that objective language about God is impossible. The consequence is that theological language is reduced to language about Jesus Christ and about man's self-understanding.

This is the group which has taken up the world-come-of-age theme of Bonhoeffer to celebrate the autonomy that they affirm characterizes true secularity. Since Christ has dethroned the "powers" to which man has been in bondage, it is the duty of Christians to set about the task of freeing men from sacred idols (e.g., false supernaturalism, sacralized society) in order that they may be truly human.

The "God is dead" and the "secular city" movements seem unlikely to have any long-term influence on theological thought, but they have touched a tender nerve in exposing the breakdown of traditional God-language as meaningful communication for our time, and the inadequacy of the church's traditional stance toward the world. The intensification of concern for the secular is likely to be a continuing theme in theology for the next decade. In the light of its traditions and stance, the Lutheran church is more likely to listen to the theological "translators" rather than "transformers" and to be more alert to the academic theologians than to the engagement theologians. Some of these approaches will be examined in greater detail in later sections of this report.

The difference between the translating and transforming approaches has been summarized by William Hordern. The contemporary concern about dialogue with the secular world has produced two major groups that threaten to split theology more decisively than any earlier theological debates. Both groups recognize the need for dialogue with the world and both attempt it. One group, however, starts with the assumption that the changes in the modern world have produced a qualitative transformation of man and his thinking. Theologians making this assumption believe that modern man can accept the Christian message only if it is changed drastically. The second group consists of theologians who admit that we live in a fast-changing world and that we must strive to translate Christian faith into terms modern men can understand. They do not agree that the essentials of Christian faith must be drastically modified.

The traditional theological stance of the Lutheran church makes crucial contemporary, continuing, intense, and systematic attention to and dialogue with the secular. In recent theology of the church there has been tension between a concept of the purpose of the church as kerygmatic and a concept of its purpose as a diakonic response to human need. In Lutheran theology this tension has been largely resolved in a view of service as the response of faith active in love. But evidence of the continuing tension in the life of the church is seen clearly in reactions to the church's involvement in social, political, and economic issues.

The secular world sets the agenda for the Lutheran Church in America in the next decade in terms of a basic question: How does the church as a whole—people, clergy, agencies—become sensitive to and involved in the world and its way of thought and life? It raises the issue of mission: What is authentic proclamation today? How does the church speak to thoroughly secularized man—man who does not have points of contact with the traditional thought-forms and language of Christian proclamation —and still maintain the authentic content of the Christian tradition? What are the necessary and valid differences between proclamation within the Christian community and the proclamation of the Christian community to the secularized world? In an increasingly centralized and organized society, how does the church speak not simply to individuals but also to government, business, and the other social structures which are the power centers of secularized society?

It raises also the issue of service: How valid are the church's varied forms of ministry in terms both of adequate expression of the church's mandate and of effectiveness in meeting the need of the world's people? What should be the church's involvement in the secular movements which have the goal of freeing people for more authentic human existence? What is the proper form of Christian "presence" in the world's efforts to help and free people? The nature of these dilemmas is expressed in Langdon Gilkey's phrase "how the church can minister to the world without losing itself."

The Lutheran Church in America must discover authentic and effective ways to keep the two emphases in proper balance: reconciliation as proclamation of the work of God in Christ, and genuine involvement in the world as an embodiment and consequence of that proclamation.

## The Importance of History

The contemporary movement from static or spatial thought-models to dynamic or relational models has been noted, emphasizing that change is a central aspect of the contemporary world. Reflecting this shift is a second major theme which permeates much contemporary theological thought: the importance inadequacy of theological formulations which assume static and of history. Our age of explosive change has made evident the unchanging shapes. The church has always been aware of change and has tried to come to terms with it, often in a sort of rearguard fight against change and its effects. Today, however, there is a serious effort to build a concept of change into theological thinking about God and the church. This is being worked at primarily through a new effort to take seriously the meaning of history.

Nineteenth-century theologians did attempt to deal with history, primarily in terms of biblical *Heilsgeschichte*. This approach was discredited in the mainstream of theological thought by the dogmatic positivism of early twentieth-century historians, with their preconceived assumptions about the possibility or impossibility of certain kinds of historic events, and by the meteoric rise of dialectical theology which tended to push history into a corner where it could do no harm. Contemporary existentialist theology also tends to accentuate the immediacy of personal experience at the expense of the past and future referents in the drama of salvation.

Much current theology reasserts the importance of historical experience. An increasing number of theologians insist that faith which is not based on historical facts can be mere subjectivism and that preaching the word of God is an empty assertion if it is severed from its historical base and content. This concern is seen clearly in the "new quest for the historical Jesus" initiated by post-Bultmannian theologians, who recognize that unless there is continuity between the historical Jesus and the proclamation of the church, there is danger of finding ourselves committed to a mythological Lord.

The most complete systematic effort so far at "taking history seriously" is seen in Wolfhart Pannenberg and the group of theologians associated with him. They affirm that revelation does not merely come *in* and *through* history, but *is* history. The totality of reality as history is God's world, which he creates and through which he reveals himself. This is opposed to a *Heilsgeschichte* in which God reveals himself only at certain times and through certain parts of history. The end of history has already occurred in Jesus of Nazareth. But the ending is still unaccomplished for most of creation, so history goes on, and the future remains open. God is the power that brings redemption in the midst of change.

Many other theologians seek to deal with history and the meaning of change. Ogden, building on the foundations of Whitehead's metaphysics, argues that God is somehow like the primary reality we know—conscious, experiencing subjectivity. Therefore, God is not immutable but involves himself in life and history. The recent school of eschatological theologians in Europe (Sauter, Metz, Moltmann) sees God as the pressure for maturity and responsibility exerted on man by an unequivocally open future. Leslie DeWart, a Canadian Roman Catholic philosopher, argues that we must "dehellenize" Christian theology by jettisoning the entire metaphysical framework in which our idea of God is housed. The static idea, for example, of God's omnipotence would be transformed into a belief in "the radical openness of history—in a belief that the world is totally open to God and therefore totally open to future creation by man." God, he insists, has taken up permanent residence in history, and he is that presence within history which is not a part of history but makes history possible. Teilhard de Chardin's thoroughgoing effort to express Christian thoughts in terms of scientific evolutionary theory continues to exert considerable influence. Schillebeekx describes the church as the fulfillment of whatever is going on in society—people who try to take change seriously and bring to perfection through God all that is going on in the world. The theologians of engagement, of course, assume Gods presence and activity in history as they seek to find out "where the action is."

A similar concern for history is seen in areas beyond systematic theology. The Protestant-Catholic debate about Scripture and tradition is mitigated not only by increased Catholic interest in the Bible, but also by increasing Protestant appreciation of the meaning and value of tradition. In biblical studies the historical-critical method is here to stay, with its recognition that the revelation of God in the Bible cannot be understood apart from the historical setting in which it came to be. The historical-hermeneutical approach is applied to systematic theology. Thus Dillenberger notes that the hermeneutical problem arises in the study of texts and documents of the past. In this study hermeneutics attempts to penetrate the intention of a document or concept in the hope that its intention might be expressed in and through and despite the contemporary cultural idiom. The consequence of a serious approach to this is evident when it is recognized that the intention of a theological statement in subsequent ages may have to be explicated in formulations that outwardly contradict the original formulation.

A clear expression of the historical viewpoint in church life is seen in the Presbyterian Confession of 1967. The contemporary situation in the United Presbyterian Church is an illustration of what many confessional denominations face. The historical study of theology has been a part of Presbyterian theological education for at least twenty years, and there are now many leaders who view the Westminster Confession as only one of a series of creedal statements about our Christian faith. A committee appointed by the General Assembly to study its standards of belief presented—after eight years of study—to the General Assembly a report which historicizes their whole confessional stance. This was done by affirming a tradition that contains the Apostles' Creed and exhibits a series of creedal statements, including a new one that is to be known by its date, the Confession of 1967. This historical approach, as represented by a whole book of confessions rather than by the one Westminster Confession of Faith, makes the historical approach official in that denomination. The debate within the United Presbyterian Church over this proposed confession illustrates clearly the difficulties faced by the church in using and interpreting the historical viewpoint. Although its opponents have concentrated their attacks on the confession's abandonment of a literal interpretation of the Bible, they have also recognized that this proposal represents a radical change in the nature of the United Presbyterian Church's stance regarding confessional statements.

The contemporary emphasis on the importance and meaning of history and change must also be taken seriously by the Lutheran Church in America. There does not seem to be at the present time any desire within the Lutheran Church in America to follow the example of the United Presbyterian Church by writing a new confession of faith. The present tendency seems to be to accept the statement of the historic faith confessed in Article I of the LCA Constitution, and to interpret that confession through such channels as policy statements of LCA boards and commissions and the LCA Manifesto, which serves to express in contemporary (and temporary) form present understandings of that confession. It seems likely that ecumenical discussions (within LCUSA, with other denominational heritages, with the Roman Catholic church) will produce further clarification of the Lutheran position regarding confessional statements.

In this process the Lutheran Church in America must come to an understanding of what it means to be a confessional church in a world of change. The problem seems to be one of finding ways to maintain our Christian identity and the integrity of our historical rootage without assuming a static position or a confessional rigidity which is not open to God's continuing action and revelation in history. A critical question is the place of the Augsburg Confession in the life of the church. How is the hermeneutical principle properly applied so that the essential elements of the confession are maintained in a relevant way without the necessity of viewing the Confession itself as a depository of inviolate doctrines? Pannenberg suggests that it is not possible to present Luther's thoughts or those of the confessional writings as solutions for our present problems as a so-called "Reformation theology." In a changed situation traditional phrases, even when recited literally, do not mean the same thing that they meant at the time when they were formulated. A repristination of the language or thoughts of biblical writings is always an indication that theology has evaded the problems of its own time and thus has not accomplished what Paul, John, and Luther each accomplished for his own time.

A more practical but equally important question is how the church's theologians can participate in an influential way in the formulation of the policy statements and program elements which in effect shape or express the church's contemporary confessional stance. In its ongoing life at the congregational level the church has an obligation to undertake the massive effort required to help lay people move toward a historical view of theology and the Bible, and away from an expectation of a theology which absolutizes both the questions and answers. We must find ways to help people move toward an understanding of the intention of historical, biblical, and theological statements. This is no simple task, since it requires that people learn to live without the supposed assurance provided by "final" theological answers. It requires basic study to determine the processes involved in "thinking theologically," so that the church can help lay people do at their own level what the theologian does at a more sophisticated level—to reflect on the meaning of existence in the light of the historical community and the contemporary world.

## Contemporary Theological Approaches

In spite of these key themes which cut through much current theological thought, it is evident that contemporary theology is in a state of flux. Different theologians tend to handle even these common themes in radically different ways. The old schools of thought are breaking down, but the form of new schools has not yet taken shape. It is impossible to predict the specific forms which the theology of the 1970's will take. However, just as it is possible to identify certain common concerns which will almost certainly be of central importance for both theology and the church, so, too, it is possible to identify certain contemporary theologians and schools of theology whose work must be taken seriously by the LCA in its thoughts and planning. None of them are entirely new—all have roots in traditional and recent theological thinking. For the most part they are described below in terms of thought of one contemporary theologian who seems of central importance. Some of the implications of these theological trends for the LCA are indicated. In the sections that follow we will deal with seven current theological approaches:

Conservative theology
Reformation theology
Existentialist theology
Theology and history
Theology and process philosophy
Theology and organic evolution
Theology and world religions

## II. CONSERVATIVE THEOLOGY

Still a potent theological force in the life of the church is conservative theology. After the defeat of fundamentalism in one battle after another in the theological wars of the twenties and thirties, its imminent demise was freely predicted. Such death notices, however, proved to be premature. Out of the ashes has arisen what William Hordern calls "the new face of conservatism"—a self-conscious program of scholarship that seeks a statement and defense of Christian orthodoxy with intellectual rigor. (It must be noted that the "Christian orthodoxy" being explicated is that of the sixteenth- and seventeenth-century Protestant confessions, especially the Reformed.)

Fundamentalism of the 1920's was not essentially a movement of theological scholarship. It was primarily a popular defense against social and intellectual change and the supposed heresies of modernism and liberal Christianity. Although expressed in a variety of ways, its basic tenets were belief in the inerrancy and plenary inspiration of the Bible as God's word with an objectively definable content and insistence on a traditionally supernatural worldview with an uncompromising emphasis on miracles.

The new face of conservatism brings to each of these concerns fresh thinking and competent scholarship, something sorely lacking in fundamentalism past and present. Current conservative theology conceives itself as conservative without being reactionary. It insists that at the same time theology addresses itself to the questions and situation of modern man, it must reckon with what the Scriptures actually are and say by their own standards. It has made some beginning at developing a social ethic derived from Scripture and related to man's present needs.

Conservative theology has taken an honest look at nonconservative theology, and many of its leaders take seriously what they see. Most of them accept the work of lower criticism, and many recognize higher criticism as an important study worthy of encouragement. Conservatives are among the enthusiastic supporters of the new quest for the historical Jesus. This is accompanied by a recognition that historical research will never be able to satisfy the needs of a living faith, which comes alone from the assurances of the gospel.

Even the old notion of inerrancy, the conservatives' most difficult problem, is changing. The old-style fundamentalist argued that to deny the truth of any statement of Scripture was to call God a liar. The conservative is more inclined to argue that the man who denies inerrancy falls into contradiction or confusion. Conservative theologians recognize the possibility of errors creeping into the Scripture, but insist that the Holy Spirit would not permit any that would imperil man's salvation. In the same manner of thinking, they admit that there may be errors in the record of historical events recorded in Scripture, but maintain that accounts of those main events in which God shows himself and through which he saves are true and without error. This encompasses the events recorded in the Gospels, including the stories of the miracles.

Conservatism sees itself as a corrective to modern theology in a number of ways. By its insistence that the Bible contains not only the record of God's mighty acts but God's own interpretation of those acts, it sees itself as saving us from the difficulty of recognizing a God who can act but not speak. It also sees itself playing a corrective role in the tension between religion and science. It has worked hard at bringing science and the Bible together, and some conservative theologians have accepted a form of evolutionary theory. The conservatives insist that modern theologians have swallowed the scientific worldview without recognizing that a worldview can scarcely be a finding of science, since it rests upon metaphysical underpinnings well outside the causal nexus within which the reality acknowledged by science abides. Theology works with an additional set of "givens" within which God is conceived as free and not suppressed under the lid science clamps upon the world.

To predict the future of any line of theological thought is a hazardous game. Hordern sums up prospects for the new face of conservatism in his observation that a new conservatism has emerged from a moribund fundamentalism. The important questions are whether the acids of modernity will so corrode the leaders of this movement that they will become simply a slightly conservative expression of modern theology; whether this movement will produce a powerful successor to Barth's theology; whether the liberal trend of Protestant theology in general will leave a vacuum in the theological center that will be filled by the new conservatism; whether the new conservatives will prove to be closer and more relevant to the laity and their problems than are more sophisticated theologies; whether the new conservatives are the Indian summer of fundamentalism.

The implications of conservative theology must be considered at two levels—in terms of the church's theological thought and in terms of the life of its congregations. Glock and Stark classify the Lutheran Church in America among the more conservative denominations (together with the American Lutheran Church, the American Baptist Convention, and, in some senses, the Roman Catholic church). Two points need to be made about this classification: it is based on questionnaire studies of *lay* church members, and it is a point on a continuum ranging from the quite liberal to a very conservative approach.

While the LCA as a whole may occupy a mid-point on such a continuum, it seems unlikely that creative or innovative theological thought for the LCA will come from the new conservative school of theology. The LCA has already left the conservative view of the Bible, accepting "the new light shed on God's Word and world by sound scholarship" (Manifesto) and discarding a rigid verbal-infallibility view of the Bible. While the LCA is deeply aware of its roots in Reformation theology, it seems unlikely to settle for a simple restatement or repristination of sixteenth-century theological thought.

The church cannot afford, however, to ignore the major concerns of conservative theology. Liberals have tended to be polite to conservatives, but to ignore them as having nothing to say worth listening to. Conservatives have tended to loose bitter blasts at liberals, but have at least paid careful attention to developments in contemporary theological thought. If we are to remain in organic continuity with our heritage, this heritage cannot simply be written off. John Dillenberger has pointed out that theological formulations of a given period cannot claim absolute validity for their own time or for subsequent periods. On the other hand, outright rejection of theological formulations of the past simply because they do not fit in the current cultural setting shows lack of awareness of one's contemporary cultural conditioning. Acceptance of theological propositions as absolute truth and rejection of theological propositions as utterly irrelevant and untrue stem from a similar mentality.

Chief among the concerns of conservative theology which must be preserved and restated in new forms is a strong sense of the importance and authority of the biblical tradition. Fundamentalists insisted that to admit error at any point in the Bible leads inevitably to a weakening of the entire authority of the Bible. The presentation of contemporary biblical scholarship does have this result for some lay people. The church must seek more effective ways to help its people read the Bible in the light of modern scholarship as a living expression of the revelation of God in history.

The conservative movement also has a strong sense of the importance of the institutional church. Although the fundamentalist attempt to gain institutional control over the major Protestant churches was defeated in the late 1920's, the very vigor of that attack was evidence of the importance which the movement attributed to the institution. This view stands in strong contrast to the anti-institutionalism and denigration of the organized church typical of many contemporary radical theologians. While there is little possibility that Lutherans will fall prey to the "no church" movement, the Lutheran view of institutional structures as adiaphora tends to discourage consideration of the institution as an empirical reality and serious examination of the validity of its structures as vehicles for missions. However, the importance of institutional forms ought not to be minimized. Glock and Stark point out that the most active and influential members of congregations tend to hold a more traditional or conservative theology, and they suggest that if a denomination is going to adopt new theological forms, it may well have to find new structural and ritual expressions or risk settling for a less significant role in the lives of men.

The third important element of conservative Christianity has been its strong sense of Christian identity. This sense is too often expressed in withdrawal from the world rather than in constructive involvement in society. The traditional conservative expressions of commitment to Christian identity—abstinence from drinking, smoking, card playing, theater attendance; Sunday-keeping and regular attendance at worship; family devotions—have largely deteriorated today, and no correspondingly distinctive Christian style of life has yet emerged to take its place. There does not seem to be within the Lutheran Church in America any group or agency which is responsible for continuing thought and action in this area. Perhaps the experience of world missions in developing indigenous Christian communities in other cultures can provide background and guidance for "indigenizing" the gospel to American culture—finding within American culture a distinctive style of life which is an authentic expression of historic Christian commitment.

## III. REFORMATION THEOLOGY

Lutheran Reformation theology is undoubtedly the core or the most typical theological formulation accepted by the majority of Lutheran Church in America clergy and laymen. That this is the case is the result of seminary training, continuing theological education, and educational literature and materials provided for both clergy and laity. Reformation theology has provided the framework for seminary courses in systematic theology and has been used as background for such courses as history of doctrine, biblical studies, church history, and catechetics. Laymen have been exposed to this way of thinking through the formal educational program and materials of the church, books and periodicals prepared for sale to laymen, and the point of view which informs most of the preaching in the LCA.

Lutheran Reformation theology has been presented and continues to exist in the church in many variant forms. The dominant contemporary interpretation of Reformation theology is well represented in the work of scholars such as Martin J. Heinecken, George Forell, William H. Lazareth, and Jaroslav Pelikan. In addition, widespread seminary use of works by Scandinavian Lutheran theologians such as Aulén, Nygren, Prenter, Wingren, and Vajta has tended to make their insights influential in the thought of American Lutherans. The "Luther renaissance" and current interest in Luther and the Reformation beginnings of contemporary Protestantism have helped to overcome many earlier misconceptions about Reformation theology.

Many factors, however, in the North American theological scene have tended to interfere with an accurate understanding of the intentions of Luther and his contemporaries. American Lutherans have been influenced by the dominant forms of American Protestant theology and have tended to assimilate these viewpoints into their concept of Lutheran theology. This tendency has been much stronger among pastors and laymen than among theologians and seminary professors. Probably the strongest influences have been those of pietism and conservative Protestant theology. Pietistic viewpoints have diluted the Reformation emphasis on "by grace alone" and have eroded the distinctive Lutheran doctrine of the church. Conservative Protestant theology has undergirded a tendency among the laity toward a form of fundamentalism with regard to the Bible and a blurring of the distinction between God's work of creation and redemption. Pietism and conservative Protestantism have influenced not only the theological viewpoints of pastors and people, but have also exerted strong influences on worship and other expressions of Christian faith and life in congregations.

Lutherans in North America have also been influenced by European schools of thought. "Lutheran orthodoxy," which flourished in Europe in the seventeenth and eighteenth centuries, has had a longer life in North America than it has in Europe. Until quite recently it was a major influence on American Lutheran theologians and seminary professors. It still survives in strength in some sections of the church. More recently American interpretations of Lutheran theology were colored by an existentialist point of view stemming from Kierkegaard, and a neo-orthodox point of view originating in Barth. These viewpoints were influential in the 1940's and 1950's. Consequently, many pastors now in or approaching the prime years of their ministry were educated in these viewpoints and are still strongly influenced by them.

Within the last several years new theological viewpoints have gained in strength and tend to be associated (at least loosely) with contemporary Lutheran theology. They include the formulations made by Reinhold Niebuhr, Emil Brunner, Paul Tillich, Rudolf Bultmann, Dietrich Bonhoeffer and Joseph Sittler. These theological interpretations have had a long-enough history and sufficient public notice to insure some influence on the thinking of a significant number of pastors and, through them, on the thinking of the laity. More recently, viewpoints of such European Lutheran theologians as Wolfhart Pannenberg and Gerhard Ebeling have received notice in American Lutheran theological journals and presumably are exerting an influence on professional theologians and, to a limited extent, on parish pastors. Parish pastors are more likely to be currently influenced by American "engagement theology" because of the widespread notice it has received.

In summary, it seems reasonable to believe that Lutheran

Reformation theology is the dominant theological viewpoint of American Lutherans. At the same time it must be recognized that it exists in the church in many variant forms because of the strong historical influences of American Protestant tradition and European theological thought upon the life of the church.

## Major Features of Reformation Theology

Lutheran theology since the time of the Reformation has placed strong emphasis on an affirmation of Christian tradition. It is thoroughly Christocentric in its emphasis on the importance of the Scriptures and the importance of doctrine. These features have produced a high degree of faithfulness to the explicitly evangelical content of the Christian witness and Christian identity. Erosion of the specifically Christian content of the faith has been resisted. This stance has enabled Lutherans to maintain a stability, a continuity of Christian witness, by avoiding extreme shifts of viewpoint which changing theological fashions can occasion. At the same time it has been possible to recognize the value of some insights offered by new theological formulations and to utilize them. For example, the strong Lutheran emphasis on the importance of the Bible has been accompanied by a recognition of the values of recent and current critical biblical scholarship. Maintenance of the Christian tradition combined with openness to valid new insights places the Lutheran church in a strategic position in the ecumenical movement. It can provide a natural point of contact between Lutheranism, Roman Catholicism, and conservative Protestantism. It can provide a healthy corrective to the tendency of some inter-Protestant unity efforts to minimize the importance of doctrine and to lose a sense of the distinctiveness of Christian identity and Christian witness.

At times distortions or misunderstandings of the Lutheran adherence to Christian tradition have produced undesirable effects. An emphasis on intellectually "correct" doctrinal formulations has sometimes inhibited valid and vital expressions of

Christian faith and life within Lutheranism. Preoccupation with the verbal formulations of doctrine which developed in the Reformation period has sometimes interfered with an understanding of their substance and contemporaneously relevant expressions of that substance. Sociological as well as theological factors have created a strong historical-cultural conditioning among Lutherans, which makes it difficult for them to appreciate the contributions which other communions can make to contemporary expressions of Christian identity and Christian witness. Valid and justifiable awareness of ties among Lutherans has led to a deep concern for Lutheran unity which sometimes interferes with the articulation and expression of such unity as exists between Lutherans and Christians of other communions.

One of the major contributions of Lutheranism to theological understandings ever since the Reformation has been a recognition of the difference between the realm of creation and the realm of redemption. It has been expressed in many ways: the emphasis on salvation by grace alone through faith alone; the recognition of the "hiddenness" of God in creation and his revelation of himself in Christ; the concept of the Christian as a redeemed sinner *simul justus et peccator*. This viewpoint is consistent with the two concepts of eschatology which interpenetrate one another in the New Testament—the concept that the kingdom of God has come in the life, death, and resurrection of Christ and the concept that the kingdom is yet to be consummated in fulness. The Reformation insight does justice to the two ways that humans perceive God's action and is thus congruent with a personal-existential interpretation of Christianity which communicates meaningfully to many people. It guards against diluting the content of the divine-human relationship, a phenomenon which occurs when all experiences and aspects of life are considered to be in some sense redemptive.

When the distinction between creation and redemption is properly understood, it provides a basis for full participation by Christians in the life of society without the evils which accompany theocratic doctrines or ecclesiastical domination of society. It provides a theological impetus for action in society. The distinction between creation and redemption gives a measure of independence to life in society which militates against legalism while at the same time maintaining a sense of responsibility which guards against antinomianism. The values of the distinction are evident in such specific formulations as the LCA's Board of Social Ministry statement on church-state relationships, in which the proper relationship is described as "institutional separation" and "functional interaction."

Misunderstandings and distortions of the distinction between creation and redemption have sometimes produced unfortunate consequences in the life of the Lutheran church. There has sometimes been a tendency to consider creation unimportant and redemption all-important. When this has happened, the result has been a lack of social consciousness, a tolerance of injustice in the world, a tendency to support the status quo. Privatism and quietism have been symptoms of the tendency to separate religion from the life of the Christian in the world.

Much contemporary theological opinion is inconsistent with the traditional Lutheran distinction between creation and redemption. Serious efforts are needed to discover ways of preserving the values of this insight and reinterpreting it in a fashion which validates it in the context of the contemporary intellectual climate.

A healthy contact with and interpretation of reality has enabled the Lutheran church and Lutheran theology to utilize valid insights developed in various fields of human endeavor. Lutheran theology has been able to incorporate valuable insights from biblical scholarship, historical study of the confessions, existential and neo-orthodox theology. The concept of *adiaphora* helps Christians and the church avoid overcommitment to nonessentials. Lutheran realism allows, even encourages, a healthy measure of pragmatism. It allows no rosy optimism or idealism to obscure a realistic appraisal of the nature of the empirical life of the church or the power of sin in the lives of individuals and of the world.

This healthy realism has sometimes produced an attitude of futility about efforts to improve human life, a too-ready acceptance of evils in the status quo, an unjustified exaggeration of the unimportance of life in this world. It has produced skepticism about mystical and ecstatic types of Christian experience and cast a shadow over frankly emotional types of religious expression. Although Lutherans are becoming more aware of these shortcomings which have been inherited from the past, the struggle to overcome them has not yet been completely successful.


## IV. EXISTENTIALIST THEOLOGY

Current trends in theology cannot be understood apart from a consideration of existentialist theology, since many of these trends are either rooted in or a reaction against this type of theology. Existentialism has been an influence in theology ever since Kierkegaard's revolt against philosophies which reduce the individual to "a paragraph within a system."

Starting as do many contemporary theologians with the problem of hermeneutics, Rudolf Bultmann raised a storm during World War II when he published a major article, "New Testament and Mythology." From this base, he and the scholars associated with him have developed a major theological approach based on two foundations: the form-critical method of biblical interpretation and existentialist philosophy. Bultmann's approach to biblical criticism and his characterization of the New Testament as "proclamation" (*kerygma*) are contributions of permanent value and are discussed in greater detail in a later section of this paper. Here the focus is on the existentialist approach to theology.

The central elements of this approach have been lucidly described by MacQuarrie. He points out Bultmann's position that a religious document intends to present to the reader a possibility of existence, an understanding of his own being. The document's essential meaning does not lie in the record of historical facts it may contain, not in the worldview it may reflect. It is in the possibility of existence, the self-understanding, the way of life it presents to the reader. If a document is properly explained and interpreted by asking questions appropriate to the intention of that document, a religious document such as the New Testament proves to be concerned with the questions of our own existence. What does this mean for me? What possibility of existence does it present? What understanding of my own being does it bring to me? This is the core of the existential approach to the New Testament and to the questions of theology in general.

Certain verbal distinctions are essential to understanding Bultmann's thought. He makes a crucial distinction between existential and *existentiell*. Philosophy can describe authentic life as an existential possibility. Bultmann says that we must come to the Bible with a "prior understanding" of what the writer is talking about in order to understand the "life moment" of the writer. We must be able to raise the right questions about "human being." There is no point in asking the New Testament about "what actually happened" because the writer was attempting to present not historical facts but a "possibility for existence." Bultmann believes that Heidegger's existentialist philosophy provides an analysis of human nature which is in harmony with the New Testament, and thus provides a useful sources for the "right" questions as well as a useful language in which to express the Christian understanding for modern man. Philosophy, however, only describes human possibilities, it does not give the person the power to make the choice that leads to authentic life. God's act in Christ reveals to each man the fact that he is loved by God and therefore gives him the *existentiell* freedom to love.

A second critical distinction is between *Historie* and *Ge-*

*schichte.* History consists of two layers: the historical facts that can be objectively established (*Historie*) and the existential meanings that make a demand on me for decision and commitment (*Geschichte*). For Bultmann, Christian faith lies primarily in the realm of *Geschichte*. It does not depend on the investigations of historians; it is a matter of personal response to the church's preaching of Christ—man's response to the past as it lives for him today as he enters into it with decision.

These verbal distinctions underlie Bultmann's program of "demythologization." The Bible comes to us in a framework of myth which is unintelligible to modern man. Its purpose is not to give an objective picture of the world but to express man's self-understanding. Hence we cannot simply eliminate myth, as the nineteenth-century liberal theologians tried to do. We must instead interpret the myths existentially so that they call modern man to a decision about his own self-understanding and existence. Bultmann seeks to discover a meaning of permanent value clothed in the form of the myth. He believes that buried in the strange language of the New Testament lies a *kerygma*, a proclamation of a way of life by which men can understand themselves and for which they can decide. If the proclamation is not discerned, the myth is like a husk without a kernel. It is meaningless. When the meaning has been understood, the myth gives a new understanding. Its concrete imagery may convey a more dynamic representation of the essential ideas which it contains than a translation into existential statements. Although the method is called "demythologizing," this must be understood as interpretation of myth and the re-expression of its content, not its simple elimination.

Bultmann and his successors have pointed out clearly the necessity for theology to be carried out as an expression of faith within the context of the believing community, in contrast to the supposed objectivity of some earlier continental theologians. Basic to their thought is the need for personal existential decision. We cannot base our faith on correct knowledge of facts but on our decision for or against authentic life as revealed by the proclamation of these facts (or myths). We cannot speak of God "objectively" apart from our personal involvement.

Bultmann and his followers have also raised in unavoidable fashion the difficulty of communicating the gospel to contemporary man. He is undoubtedly right when he says that modern man often cannot hear the gospel because the form in which it is presented is unintelligible to him. However, a question may be raised about whether existentialist categories are any more intelligible to contemporary man than the ancient biblical mythologies which they are supposed to interpret.

The problem of contemporary understanding of the existentialist position is seen clearly in Bultmann's approach to the historical Jesus. He has argued that the quest for the historical Jesus is both impossible and illegitimate: impossible because the necessary data are not available, and illegitimate because it is an effort to prove faith, to escape the demand for decision and belief without any guarantee from the results of scholarship. For this reason he tends to dismiss the historical Jesus and even the historicity of the Resurrection as irrelevant—a viewpoint which is probably incomprehensible to the majority of American people with their pragmatic empiricist approach.

Bultmann's radical division of history into two dimensions—history and *kerygma*—has been widely criticized. This is a split which many agree theology cannot tolerate and which is difficult for modern man to understand or accept. More basic is the criticism of the reductionism apparently inherent in the existentialist approach. Biblical mythology always has a historic character and setting. Existentialist demythologizing tends to lose this historical element and to result in an unhistorical gnosticism. It tends to reduce the theological object to man's religiousness rather than to God as transcendent referent. Thus, while existentialist theology takes seriously the importance of communicating to the secular world, it seems to move away from a serious concern for God's involvement in the historical dimension of reality and to move toward a personal subjectivism which may be characterized as a new form of pietism.

Gerhard Ebeling, the successor to Emil Brunner at the University of Zurich, is considered one of the foremost "post-Bultmannians" and is modifying Bultmann's position on history. He attempts to relate the *kerygma* to its roots in the historical Jesus, while maintaining the existentialist definition of faith as an act of decision affirming the meaning of personal existence in the present moment. In spite of his efforts to relate the *kerygma* to the historical Jesus, Ebeling still maintains basically the existentialist view of the separation between faith and history and the resistance to the "objectification" of God. "God is not an objectifiable piece of reality."

Like Bultmann, Ebeling is wrestling seriously with what he considers to be the chief problem for theology: the communication of faith in the contemporary world. He has chosen to commit himself to a category gleaned from existentialist philosophy, specifically from the "I-Thou" school. This category, termed word-event or language-event, points to what has been called "the linguisticality of existence," namely, that human existence is authentic only in the consummated interpersonal confrontation which eventuates in the spoken communication in which two selves give themselves to the other in openness, courage, and service. Ebeling has used this category as a key for interpreting the biblical faith, Christ, the word of God, the essence of the Reformation, the significance of historical criticism, and the meaning of *sola scriptura* and *sola fide*. Ebeling believes that this category enables the Christian faith to speak honestly in the face of the relativity that permeates the contemporary world-view, because it asserts a truth-claim that is impervious to the truth-eroding character of *Geschichtlichkeit*.

For Ebeling, the basis of faith lies in Jesus as the witness of faith. What uniquely came to expression in Jesus was faith. To believe in Jesus means to re-enact the decision of faith which Jesus originally made. Faith is not a partial act; it is the whole man in openness to the future, living in relation to other men and sharing in the love of God. The church is considered to be "the summons of faith." To be in the church is to hear, respond, and share in the summons to faith, which is in turn to share in God's work. Ebeling feels that the task of hermeneutics is not, as in Bultmann, to go behind the language of a text to the understanding of existence which it enshrines; it is rather to reflect on the process by which the text becomes proclamation, a new linguistic occurrence of the word of God.

## V. THEOLOGY AND HISTORY

In contrast to the existentialist approach is the effort of Wolfhart Pannenberg, a systematic theologian of the University of Mainz, who, together with a group of younger men, insists that kerygma means nothing without history. Faith cannot depend on a kerygma divorced from its historical basis, for the kerygma itself is the declaration of what God has done in the actual course of historical events. According to Pannenberg, both Barth and Bultmann have replaced historical reason with faith and thereby have robbed theology of its attempt to express the faith in intelligible terms. He recognizes that the present situation faces us with the problem of relativity, but he points out that it also faces us with the necessity of rationally demonstrating the truth of Christianity. He attempts to meet the demand for rational demonstration by using the methodology of scientific historiography. Pannenberg insists that the claims of the Christian community must be investigated according to the methodology of the scientific historian; he is willing to abide by the results of this methodology and is confident that the basic claims of the church can withstand any probing of the historian. The historical approach is essential, for theology in speaking of God deals with all of life and history. It cannot be confined to the task of simply interpreting the Scriptures or dealing with the supernatural side of a realm of special religious revelation as distinct from so-called natural knowledge. For if the realm of the "natural" changes and becomes autonomous, then theology can only develop into the science of an "unrevelatory revelation."

The breakthrough to such a universality is necessary because the starting point of revelation theology itself, namely, the Scripture-principle, leads to the question of universal history. To understand everything as part of a universal history is to understand all things in relation to the God of the Bible, thus to understand the God of the Bible as the creator of the world. The God of the Bible is the God of history; the understanding of the world as history is the interpretation of reality which the biblical concept of God opens to mankind.

Rejecting the assumption that the theological "game" is to be played by its own special set of rules (that is, that the rules of scientific inquiry or the criteria of scientific truth do not apply, or apply somewhat differently in theology), Pannenberg sets out by affirming that: (1) the data of the Christian faith, including the central datum of the Resurrection, can and must be subjected to the same kind of vigorous historical scrutiny that would be brought to bear on any event in history; and (2) historical truth is organically one and cannot be separated into "revealed" and "scientific" truth or into "saving" and "secular" history. When the biblical writers spoke of God's involvement in history, they meant *all* of history as they knew it. So it is demanded that theology take seriously all currents and periods in history as being organically inseparable. The whole is relevant: "golden ages" and "special histories" are emphatically disallowed.

The Pannenberg viewpoint strongly objects to separating history into mere facts on the one hand and human meaning on the other. Responsible historiography sees fact and meaning in indissoluble connection. Faith is an appropriate response to the meaningful factual history of God's revelation.

History in its totality is the revelation of God. The Bible expresses the progressive discovery of the unity and comprehensiveness of revelation, culminating in the universalism of apocalypticism. At every stage prophecy is fulfilled in unexpected ways. Jesus proclaimed a universal resurrection as the end of history. His prophecy was vindicated by his own Resurrection and thus provides the key to the meaning of all history as revelation.

As John Cobb indicates, Pannenberg sees the historicity of the Resurrection as a crucial issue for theology. Positivistic historians had operated on the basis of an evolutionary and naturalistic worldview which saw history as an unbroken chain of interconnections of cause and effect. This view led to certain assumptions about what could and could not be "historical." Existentialist theology accepted this view of history ("An historical fact which involves a resurrection from the dead is utterly inconceivable"—Bultmann) but took refuge in an interpretation of the gospel records as expressions of faith and of a new self-understanding of existence.

A number of theologians have made a direct attack during the past decade on the mechanistic and positivistic assumptions of this view of history. Moltmann has shown how modern preconceptions of what is historically possible stand in direct contradiction to the biblical view of historical possibility. In the Bible historical reality is open to the activity of God. Modern ideas of historical possibility and probability have been developed in complete indifference to the biblical picture of God as the subject of history. If only the "humanly possible" is historical, then the resurrection of Jesus is both impossible and meaningless. The procedure can be reversed. It is possible to define history in the light of the reality of Jesus' resurrection. When this is done, the historical question of the reality of Jesus' resurrection turns back upon the inquiring historian and calls into question the presuppositions about history which he uses in his historical inquiry.

Pannenberg insists that the Resurrection is the primary datum of the church's faith and that faith stands or falls upon the historical verification of this event. The resurrection of Jesus is absolutely decisive for any Christian proclamation and for the Christian faith itself. Jesus' resurrection is the basis of faith, but this cannot owe its certitude to a decision of faith, otherwise faith would find its basis in itself. Thus Paul in 1 Corinthians 15 did not think a mere demand for faith was enough. He gave a list of witnesses of the resurrection of Jesus. Such a proof was commonly used in legal proceedings. Paul gave a historical proof, a firsthand proof beyond doubt.

The Resurrection is of special importance in establishing the link between the historical Jesus and the kerygma of the church —the problem with which the post-Bultmannians have been wrestling. The Christian faith cannot be based on the pre-Easter Jesus, for "such Christology—and the proclamation based upon it—would be reduced to an empty assertion." On the other hand, a kerygma unrelated to the historical Jesus is mere superstition. The question of the continuity between the kerygma and the historical Jesus cannot be grasped unless one grasps the connection between Jesus' own claim to authority and God's vindication of that claim by raising him from the dead.

Jesus is the final revelation of God; therefore, he himself is God. This doctrine adds nothing essential to the resurrection of Jesus; it only makes clear the meaning of that event. Pannenberg in a tightly reasoned argument insists that the Resurrection can stand as the most reliable interpretation of the events that have engendered the Christian confessions.

Pannenberg also deals with the problem of hermeneutics. He agrees that the problem is that of expressing a given content in a completely changed situation. But, in contrast to others, he believes that interpretation must be a two-way street. It is not simply a matter of adapting the tradition to contemporary thought-patterns, but also of seeking a "merging of horizons" through which contemporary thought may also be influenced by the tradition. This difficulty can be overcome only if we succeed in bringing contemporary thought again into a more explicit connection with Christian tradition. It is not sufficient simply to adapt Christian tradition to opinions current in our time. Nor is it possible to transform our present intellectual world into that of the first Christian century. But perhaps the Christian tradition can contribute to the development of modern thought. The present may be related to early Christianity in terms of the horizon of the historical process. The hermeneutical difference between the transmitted text and our present time is at once respected and superseded in a concept of the history connecting both, if this history can be regarded as the work of the biblical God.

Pannenberg's approach requires taking seriously the eschatological reality of the Christian testimony. Precisely here is located the foundation of all that is said about the unity of history in which God is active. Only in this eschatological anticipation, this *hope*, can Christian theology speak of history as a whole.

Based on *Offenbarung als Geschichte*, Braaten summarizes Pannenberg's position in seven propositions:

A. According to biblical witnesses, the self-revelation of God has occurred indirectly through historical acts.

B. Revelation occurs, not at the beginning, but at the end of history.

C. Unlike special manifestations of God, historical revelation can be seen by all; it is universal in character.

D. The universal revelation of the Godhead was not realized in the history of Israel, but first in Jesus of Nazareth insofar as the end of history exists in him.

E. The Christ-event does not reveal the God of Israel as an isolated event, but only as part of God's history with Israel.

F. The universality of the eschatological self-disclosure of God in the destiny of Jesus was expressed by using non-Jewish ideas of revelation in the instruction of Gentile Christians.

G. The Word of revelation is given in terms of prophecy, instruction, and report.

Pannenberg's thinking so far has had relatively little influence in American theology, primarily because his writings are only beginning to be translated into English. On the other hand, Pannenberg seems to be influenced by American theology. He is experimenting with an adaptation of process theology as a kind of metaphysical explanation of his view of history. In a lecture at the University of Pennsylvania he spoke of God as "the power of the future," apparently an incorporation of Whitehead's process metaphysics with an eschatological motif.

Pannenberg's position is likely to become more important as it develops in the future. Although some would say that he cannot speak to modern man because he speaks of God, he is alert to the currents of contemporary thought. Working from the starting point and within the methodology of scientific historiography, he speaks in a way that makes sense to many modern men. Of equal importance is his sense of the importance, continuity, and integrity of the Christian position. He speaks unapologetically as one who is ready for real dialogue with the world, in contrast to the "transformers" whose criterion for modern theology is what "modern man" can accept. He feels that theology can do more than simply accept the place where man stands today; it can question his standing place and tell the world something that the world is not telling itself (as seen in his criticism of historiographic assumptions). His framework of universal history is broad enough to encompass the restatement of all the traditional concerns of theology, particularly the currently crucial issues of hermeneutics and eschatology. Acceptance of his approach may result in less emphasis on the irrational and paradoxical (without implying a return to nineteenth-century rationalism) and more concern for the wholeness of the biblical witness and Christian history.

## VI. THEOLOGY AND PROCESS PHILOSOPHY

Natural theology has traditionally been the effort to construct a doctrine of God on the basis of experience alone without appeal to faith or special revelation. It has been a strand in theology for centuries, especially in Roman Catholic Scholasticism. In America this approach was represented by Henry Nelson Wieman and Charles Hartshorne, both of whom used Whitehead's metaphysics as foundation for a dynamic concept of God and the world as mutually necessary to each other. W. Norman Pittenger also drew on a concept of the continued and intimate relationship between God and creation in shaping his doctrine of incarnation. These earlier efforts at building a natural theology were largely overwhelmed by the Barthian and neo-orthodox reaction against nineteenth-century rationalism and liberalism.

Interest in natural theology has increased recently. Theologians such as John Cobb and Schubert Ogden have begun to explore again the implications of process metaphysics. Paul Tillich perhaps prepared the way for this renewed interest by recasting the terms of the debate. He argued that philosophy formulates the basic human questions about God rather than providing proofs or arguments for his existence. To him theology's task is to show that these questions presuppose an awareness of finitude and of being itself, and to demonstrate that the Christian symbols provide an answer to these basic human questions.

John Cobb is developing one of the most significant attempts to establish a place for natural theology in the explication of the Christian faith. He argues that the current dialogue with the world demands, not the elimination or discounting of metaphysics, but the use of a contemporary metaphysics which he finds in the thought of Whitehead and Hartshorne. He criticizes those Christians who see atheism as a useful tool for ridding faith of inappropriate superstitions or rationalistic crutches. He points out that the prevailing atheistic mentality does not stop with the rejection of this or that inadequate concept of God. It rejects any idea that involves the superhuman, and thereby also and without qualification rejects the God revealed in Jesus Christ.

The reactions that have been given to an instrumental use of atheism by theologians opposed to natural theology are that philosophic formulations are cultural phenomena that must be treated as of no fundamental importance for the gospel. Some have even thought of it as positive gain on the grounds that false ideas of God are thus destroyed and that the opportunity for the encounter with the truly transcendent God known only in Jesus Christ is heightened. This view is commonly associated with an attitude of contempt for the kind of restless questioning that marks the piety actually characteristic of the church today. Still, others have thought that the emptiness of the term "God" makes it clear that we must either cease to use this word or redefine it in terms of categories that are meaningful to modern man.

Cobb insists that the alternative reaction is to try to restore the term "God" to meaningful discourse in some real continuity with its historic use. He insists that such restoration is both useful and possible, and that it is a matter of life and death for spiritual existence as Christians that the reality of the referent of God be a part of our intellectual conviction. He does not find justification in biblical or Christian history for the view that God acts in radical independence of intellectual and cultural history. On the other hand, he asks those who believe that the gospel requires no reference to God in any sense other than special mode of human existence or togetherness whether they realize that the same cultural and intellectual forces which militate against the meaningfulness of the word "God" operate also against most of that which they continue to affirm.

The evaporation of meaning from this crucial term "God" has occurred, not as a function of that theology which is the expression of articulation of faith, but as a function of that cosmology which has destroyed the horizons within which early Christian, medieval, and early modern man understood his existence. This means that natural theology in our generation is not to be seen as the dubious luxury of the systematician, but as foundational to proclamation and to the realization of faith as well. Cobb points out that the emerging atheism of our day is rooted in highly self-conscious and reflective thought. An adequate response to its challenge must be at its own intellectual level. Modern philosophical currents oppose the renewal of belief in God and it is impossible to avoid a struggle with them. Natural theology has become, as never before in Christian history, a matter of utmost urgency for the church.

In *A Christian Natural Theology* Cobb tries to do with White-head's thought what Thomas Aquinas attempted with Aristotle's. He proposes that the process philosophy of Whitehead offers us a powerful conceptual scheme for understanding the essential teachings of Christianity. One of the interesting approaches that Cobb takes to the use of natural theology is that he asks that the philosophical system provide the fundamental vision of reality and the criteria of truth. The Christian faith is to provide topics and questions to be discussed. This approach is something of a reversal of Tillich's "method of correlation" in which the questions and concerns of existence are raised by philosophy and responded to by theology.

Cobb gives the rationale for his approach to theology by defining what he means by a Christian natural theology. By "natural" he means that his methodology uses the intellectual resources provided by process theology. He does not imply that the rational can supplant faith, but rather that the rational can give coherence and clarity to the expression of the experience of faith. By "Christian" he intends that the theologian bring to his search for truth all the concerns and questions that arise from his experience in the community of faith.

Natural theology consists of efforts of those who from a firm foundation in Christian faith think through the whole range of intellectual questions that modern man must struggle with. Such reflection must not appeal to any authority not recognized outside the church (such as Scripture, revelation, tradition or personal religious experience). It must be thoroughly open to evidence from any source, and it must unreservedly risk its own basic vision in the process. It can justify itself only by showing that Christian faith opens itself to all scrutiny in the interest of truth.

Cobb states with great emphasis that his second major intellectual endeavor is an evolutionary-historical approach to the understanding of Christian existence, arising out of reflection on the question of what it means to be a Christian, what it means to live in the community of faith and to participate in a distinctive mode of existence that is understood to have come from Jesus Christ. He insists that Christian existence is distinctive and that it depends upon Jesus Christ. He has not found existentialism a satisfactory interpretation of the meaning of human existence. He maintains that the existentialist understanding of existence is strictly that of the post-Christian Western man—an understanding that gives no cognizance to where man has been in the past, that is, the historical experience of man or the evolutionary process through which man has come.

He insists that it will become increasingly clear that the history of Israel is central to human history and that this history culminated and was transformed in Jesus Christ. He believes that it will be possible to show that Christian existence is unique and that it became a possibility for the first time in Jesus Christ. These assertions demonstrate that the theologian must take seriously his history and his tradition in which the Christ-event occurred. But he does not limit the significance of Jesus Christ simply to the past event; he is equally concerned with the fact that the Christian community and the Christian spirit eventually wither when they have no opportunity for self-renewal in repeated re-encounter with Jesus Christ. Dependence of Christian existence upon Jesus is seen not only in the fact of historical influence, but also and just as importantly in its need for conscious renewal of the relationship. Christian natural theology, in Cobb's view, is indispensable in reflection on God and his relation to the world and leads to an understanding of what it means to affirm the work of God in Jesus Christ.

Langdon Gilkey raises the same question about Cobb that others raise about Bultmann's use of existentialist philosophy: Can the Christian theologian adopt any philosophical system for the explication of the faith without making some necessary adjustments? Pannenberg finds it necessary to question some of the assumptions of scientific historiography in his approach. Gilkey cites both Augustine and Thomas Aquinas as examples of theologians who found it necessary to reconstruct the philosophical system to fit them for their Christian concepts. He maintains that Cobb has not modified Whitehead's conceptual system radically enough, that many Christian beliefs are either radically redrawn or else dispensed with in order to fit the shape and demands of the system. He maintains that Cobb's attempt to use the Whiteheadian system without adjustment does not adequately deal or come to terms with such themes as love, sin, judgment, forgiveness. He points out that the God of Whitehead's thought, who represents merely the factor of order and value within the process, is hardly a God whose mercy transcends the law and whose love fulfills the requirements of the order.

Traditional Lutheran bias against natural theology may make it difficult for us to hear Cobb, but his approach seems likely to make a significant contribution to attempts to speak to the secular world in a framework of contemporary philosophy. The following factors are of special importance: (1) the facilitation of a more creative dialogue between Christianity and other religions; (2) a serious consideration of change and God's involvement in it; (3) a renewed appreciation of the potential of human reason.

Of special importance for the Lutheran church is the re-examination of the traditional separation between nature and grace, between creation and redemption. Joseph Sittler has pointed out that the most pressing theological task today is the serious acceptance of the fact that divine grace permeates creation. He expressed his views eloquently in his *Called to Unity* address to the New Delhi Assembly of the World Council of Churches in 1961: "Enlightenment man could move in on the realm of nature and virtually take it over because grace had either ignored or repudiated it. A bit of God died with each new natural conquest; the realm of grace retreated as more of the structure and process of nature was claimed by now autonomous man. . . .

"The problem forced upon us by the events of the present decade is not soluble by the covert dualism of nature and grace. At a certain period in Christian thought and practical life, this dualism worked itself out in the dualism of church and world, of spiritual and temporal. But the time when Christian theology and Christian life could operate with such a view of things is long over. The view was never appropriate to the organic character of biblical speech; in the present state of man's knowledge in all areas it has become unintelligible. . . .

"A doctrine of redemption is meaningful only when it swings within the larger orbit of a doctrine or creation. For God's creature of earth cannot be redeemed in any intelligible sense of the word apart from a doctrine of the cosmos which is his home, his definite place, the theater of his selfhood under God, in cooperation with his neighbor, and in caring-relationship with nature, his created sister."

Daniel Day Williams has pointed out the value of process theology in serving as a bridge between biblical categories and the contemporary worldview. He notes that philosophical theology which takes process as its basic category has a powerful advantage over metaphysical systems in which Christian thought has traditionally been expressed. This philosophical framework makes it possible for the living God, the saving God of the Bible, to be made intelligible. To think of God acting in dynamic relation to his creatures as the universal creative power which sustains all things, and without which they could not be or act, is true to what our best knowledge of the world tells us. It is true to the insight of the Bible, which other philosophical traditions have tended to obscure behind an impassive mask of absolute, static being.

## VII. THEOLOGY AND ORGANIC EVOLUTION

A strikingly different approach which contains an interest in the process-dynamic of reality, is to be found in the thought of Pierre Teilhard de Chardin. Both a paleontologist and a priest, Teilhard spent most of his life in enforced isolation from the theological community and was, indeed, prohibited from publishing any work of an overtly theological nature. His main associations were, therefore, with members of the scientific community, most of whom were secular humanists, agnostics, or atheists. As a consequence, Teilhard was forced to express his basically theological concerns in secular terms. His many writings are to one degree or another exercises in intense theological reflection upon empirical reality and such widely diverse topics as automation and cybernetics, eugenics, war, and the uses of science.

Teilhard takes the theme of evolution and gives it a wholly new direction. In 1934 he began his *Comment je crois* with a credo which summarizes his phenomenological approach. He wrote that he believed the universe is an evolution, that the evolution is toward Spirit, that Spirit fulfills itself in a personal God, that the supreme personality is the Universal Christ.

Teilhard sounds a clearly optimistic note. Evolution—including human evolution—has not ceased. It is moving onward, indeed accelerating, toward its fulfillment. Every level reaches a limit of complexity. The heavier atomic elements are unstable and transitory; the most complex molecules break down unless they are taken up into a higher realm of life. Progress can continue only by periodic changes of state in which the units of one level become the component parts of higher entities. In man, evolution seems to have reached such a limit. This meant, to Teilhard, that man is approaching a new threshold—a new, critical, synthetic leap.

As at every stage in the ascent of matter-consciousness, the individual element finds its true function, the meaning of its existence, as part of a higher entity, through which it participates in a superior level of being. The individual achieves the maximum development and fulfillment of his personality in proportion as he is both nourished by and participates creatively in his culture. No evolutionary future awaits man except in his association with all other men, says Teilhard.

Just as earth once covered itself with a film of interdependent living organisms which we call the biosphere, so mankind's achievements are forming a global network of collective mind to which Teilhard gave the name "noosphere." This higher union in a complex-centered whole can be achieved only by a spontaneous inner force of attraction and cohesion. This force of mutual attraction, which unites the inner, spiritual form of energy, is love. Love, according to Teilhard, is a vital factor in a scientific picture of the universe. Like consciousness, it is not the exclusive property of living beings but has its roots in the very energy which builds atoms and molecules into self-surpassing complexes. Proto-love, like proto-consciousness, is a universal property of all matter. It is the energy of synthesis whereby matter is raised from its lowest to its highest state. Love is the very motor of evolution, bringing about the integration of individuals into higher entities.

As this comes about, Teilhard argues, evolution turns matter inside out, so to speak, transforming its physical energy into spiritual energy and its structural arrangements into that network of psychic functions we call personality. The personality which would emerge from the noosphere's centering upon itself is inconceivable, except by analogy, in terms of the individual personality known to us. Thus Teilhard speaks of "super-consciousness" or "hyper-personality," or more commonly, he designates this "pole of convergence" by the symbol "Omega."

Teilhard attributes to "Omega" those qualities which it must have if it is to be an effective as well as an ideal goal. For Omega to attract men's hopes, motivate their efforts, inspire them to sacrifice their egocentric individualism, it must be personal, loving, and lovable. The "It" must become a "Thou," to borrow Buber's expression. Moreover, Omega's attractive force must be contemporaneously present, not merely future and theoretical. It must entail, not the suppression or diminution of individual personality, but its expansion and fulfillment. Omega is not an ocean of being in which the drops lose their identity, but a "center of centers," the focus which unites a new totality within which individual centers not only retain but extend their personalities in loving relationship to all the others through personal attachment to the Supreme Center.

Teilhard feels that the advance of evolution shows that Omega is already at work, radiating the necessary love-energy, attracting the elements into more perfect union, transcending time and space, just as human thought is able to do on a lesser scale. When evolution has reached its term, when all that is capable of transformation into spirit has been gathered into a centered whole, an ultimate change of state will occur, detaching the mind, fulfilled at last, from its material matrix, so that it will henceforth rest in God-Omega.

The thought of Teilhard de Chardin is significant at this time because it provides a rich supply of hints regarding a theological understanding of unfolding reality and because it is an example of an attempt to communicate with an age which is at bottom a-theistic.

Teilhard is an example of a lifelong effort at speaking to the secular in a meaningful way. Teilhard felt that the church cannot perform her mission to the world by aiming its message only at the anxious, the introspective, or even the pious people of the world. If the gospel of Christ is to guide man's most creative and adventurous endeavors, it must reach those who are responsible for our society's economic, political, scientific, and cultural development. It was a similar concern which led Bonhoeffer to ask his now-famous questions: "How would it be possible to speak in a secular fashion of God?" "How can Christ become the Lord of those with no religion?"

In the eyes of some critics, too many such attempts to translate the gospel into secular terms have fallen into the trap of reducing Christian theology to the categories of the particular secular group to which each apology is addressed. The basic obstacle, as Bonhoeffer saw, lies in the very act of "thinking in two spheres." The task which confronts the church is not so much to translate the language of one sphere into that of another as it is to lead the inhabitants of both spheres toward a more comprehensive vision showing the limitations of either taken by itself, and to subsume them both into one overarching God-centered synthesis. Such was the task to which Teilhard set himself. He shows the same concern as Pannenberg for discovering ways in which the Christian community can say things to the world which the world is not saying to itself. His success in communication is illustrated by the fact that *The Phenomenon of Man* is probably the only theological work to have been the subject of a major book review in *The Scientific American*.

Teilhard's work was essentially an individual *tour de force*. He did not develop a "school" either around him or following him, and it is therefore difficult to predict what will be the future of his point of view. However, this effort to translate the themes of the gospel into the language of a secular discipline continues to stimulate theologians.

## VIII. THEOLOGY AND WORLD RELIGIONS

Given the increasing concern for the secular and the historical in theology, and the straining of the world toward a planetary culture, it was almost inevitable that the issues of the history of religion and of other world religions would arise.

An articulate contemporary statement on the relevance of the history of religions for Christian theology was made by Paul Tillich in his last public lecture. Mircea Eliade, the history of religions scholar at the University of Chicago, noted that it is significant and perhaps symbolic that the last public lecture of Paul Tillich was entitled "The Significance of the History of Religions for the Systematic Theologian." In that superb and moving lecture Professor Tillich declared that, were there time, he would write a new systematic theology oriented toward the whole history of religions and in dialogue with them. He felt that a new systematic theology was needed—a theology which takes into consideration the religious traditions of Asia and the primitive world, together with their recent crises and traumatic transformations, as well as the existential crisis and the religious vacuum of contemporary Western societies.

We will never know what the result of Tillich's encounter with primitive and oriental religions might have seen. It is significant that he surmised that confrontations would have a decisive role not only for Christian theology, but for the world at large. We are already approaching a planetary culture. Before long even the most provincial historian, philosopher, or theologian will be impelled to think through his problems and formulate his beliefs in dialogue with colleagues from other continents and believers in other religions.

In his last lecture, Tillich dealt with three facets of the relation between Christianity and other religions: (1) the necessity to overcome both the exclusivism of neo-orthodoxy and the new theology's rejection of the secular; (2) a basic outline of theology of the history of religion; (3) a method for interpreting theological traditions in the light of religious phenomena. He placed central emphasis on the "sacramental" basis of all religions—the universal experience of the holy within the finite. This concrete expression of experience continually tends to be eroded by demonization and attacked by the mystical and the ethical elements in religion. The whole history of religion is, in a sense, a fight for the "religion of the concrete spirit"—a fight of God against religion within religion. Critical moments in history, moments of *kairoi* in which the religion of the concrete spirit is actualized fragmentarily, continue to occur. The criterion for Christians is the event of the Cross. That which happened there also happens fragmentarily in other places, in other moments, has happened and will happen even though they are not historically or empirically connected with the Cross.

The aim of the theological system proposed by Tillich is not a union of the great religions as proposed by Toynbee or a universal Christomonism as suggested by Teilhard. His concern is that such a theology remain rooted in its experiential basis, trying to express basic experiences which are universally valid in universally valid statements. The universality of a religious statement lies in the depths of every concrete religion; it lies in openness to spiritual freedom both *from* one's own foundation and *for* one's own foundation.

This development is so recent that it is difficult to estimate how much influence it will have. John Cobb has expressed interest in it, feeling that because Whitehead's philosophy has many points of contact with the East, a natural theology utilizing Whiteheadian categories can aid the West in rethinking its faith in the light of the great religions of the East. Friedrich Heiler, the history of religion scholar at Munich and Marburg, also seems to be working along these lines.

This type of approach has not been a strand of traditional Lutheran theology, although Archbishop Söderblom maintained: "I know there is a living God, I can prove it through the history of religion." C. J. Curtis, who has made the study of Söderblom one of his chief interests, has called for the establishment of a new theological school as a relevant answer to the "God is dead" school. He maintains that a serious consideration of the world's religions would produce an enormous enrichment of contemporary philosophical theology. It will be able to achieve a world outlook which the ecumenical movement tries to create within the Christian family. The unification of philosophical theology with ecumenism promises to produce a school of the "living God" theologians who possess the wholeness of vision that the "God is dead" school seeks in vain in the debris of its own theological position.

At present this approach does not seem to be anything more systematic than a concern for considering authentic types of religious experience in other faiths and the possibility of God's action through these religions, a concern which must be shared by the Lutheran church. The question of other religions is of particular significance in world missions, as not only Christianity but also the religions of Africa and Asia have come under the attack of an autonomous secularism. If we are to come to terms with God's action in secular society, certainly we must be alert to the possibility of his activity in other religions and open to sympathetic dialogue with representatives of these faiths. Max Thurian of the Taizé community has suggested that this requires of the church, not an attitude of conquest, but one of attention and friendship. It requires, for example, the friendly presence of Christian men and women who, in silence, prayer, and friendship will share in as much of Moslem life as possible. In this way, little by little, whatever God intends from Christian and Islamic relations will be accomplished.


## IX. THEOLOGY AND MYSTICISM

A final note must be made of an aspect of contemporary theology which can hardly be categorized as a trend or school, but rather as a continuing undercurrent. This is a concern for the mystical or the paranormal. The mystical has always been a strand of Christian life, often standing in opposition to systematic theology. In Lutheranism, the choice has often seemed to be between systematic theology and an irrational pietism.

That these two elements need not be separated is seen in many areas of contemporary theology. John Cobb and Wolfhart Pannenberg illustrate the extent to which this emphasis can be found in contemporary theology. Cobb states his conviction that we should not ignore the fact that Christian believers have often—

indeed usually—known Jesus also as a personal presence. Although the absolute center of the Christian life is found in the freedom to love God and one's fellow man, the value of those experiences in which many Christians have peculiarly felt God's presence or guidance must be recognized. Although the central meaning of the sacraments is usually understood in terms of the fellowship of believers with each other and with God, the claims of a more mysterious efficacy of the sacraments should not be entirely neglected. In our effort to establish a reasonable relation between our beliefs and the dominant mentality of our day, much of value is lost. Our effort is futile unless we challenge that dominant mentality as such and do not shut ourselves off from much of the excitement and glory such as was experienced by earlier Christians.

Pannenberg agrees with Tillich that a mystical element belongs to the essence of faith. Prejudices operative in Protestantism against everything mystical must be overcome. According to the New Testament, what happened in Jesus and his resurrection is a new reality in the qualitative sense. The mystical element in faith is fellowship with Jesus and the God who appeared in him, not a general god-mysticism which has only been actualized through Jesus.

# X. CONCLUSION

It is readily apparent that any prediction as to *the* direction theology will be taking in the next decade would be the height of presumption. The great variety of experimentation with different starting points and methodologies suggests a period of creative ferment for an indefinite time to come.

Two things can be said with some definiteness. One is that contemporary theology, generally speaking, views history, "sacred" history, and the history of its own enterprise in dynamic and organic terms. Theology interacts with a host of forces and influences in the secular realm; and it also interacts with theological reflection in various forms throughout past Christian history. As to the past, it is a cumulative and self-correcting discipline; as to the future, an open-ended one.

For another thing, contemporary theology, done as it is in an increasingly ecumenical setting, is appreciating more and more that theological truth is not the discovery of one or another school or tradition, but rather that it is the result of an ongoing dialogue among the various members of the Christian "community of interpretation." No more apt a word has been spoken on this matter than that of Warren Quanbeck in a report on the ongoing interconfessional dialogue between American Calvinists and Lutherans. He notes that what is seen in the study of the Scriptures, and noted again in the development of the church's doctrine, becomes real in ecumenical discussion. It becomes apparent that Thomas Aquinas and John Calvin strived to deal with the same religious concerns, that Luther's profound sacramental realism can be complemented by Calvin's stress upon the Holy Spirit, that the entire Western tradition can learn much from Eastern Orthodox theology and spirituality. The richness and diversity of the church's tradition rooted in the Scriptures suggest the dimensions of our theological task. What is needed is a more thorough knowledge of the Scriptures, an ever-deepened understanding of the development of doctrine, a sensitivity which enables us to recognize the significance that doctrine has for worship, fellowship, service, and mission.

# 2

# Biblical Interpretation

## I. MAJOR CURRENT EMPHASES

From its beginning the church has interpreted its sacred writings. The life and teaching of the apostolic church reflect the sense of need to reexamine the Old Testament in the light of the Christ-event. The tradition that grew up in post-apostolic times rooted itself deeply in biblical interpretation. This is one of the major insights of the current assessment of the role of tradition in the life of the ancient church. The view that dogmatics should be grounded in biblical exegesis was basic in the thinking of the Reformation.

A new approach to biblical theology began with the Enlightment, which freed man's mind from the authority of scholastic systems and insisted that the Bible be put to the test of scholarly reason. Two closely related methods of inquiry evolved which have remained indispensable to biblical theology: the literary-critical method, which seeks to distinguish the work of individual authors and the original form of Scripture; and the historical method, which looks into the factors out of which biblical events and views developed. Growing out of the historical approach of the *Religionsgeschichtliche Schule* has come a new picture of the men, ideas, and institutions of biblical history. This picture has justifiably called into question earlier biblical interpretations, which were often based on a sometimes unconscious attempt to read into the biblical records the thought patterns of contemporary philosophy and theology.

The significant new element that emerged from the work of

the *Religionsgeschichtliche Schule* was the thoroughgoing effort
to split the question of meaning into two tenses: "What *did* it
mean?" and "What *does* it mean?" at least long enough for the
descriptive task to be considered by itself. This bifurcation allows
biblical scholarship to find out what the words meant when
spoken or written by the prophet, the priest, the evangelist, or
the apostle, regardless of meanings they acquired in later stages
of religious history, our own included. The task of translation
then becomes the hermeneutical effort—to state the meaning of
the biblical material for the present day.

Neither the liberals nor the conservatives of the nineteenth
century kept the distinction between the descriptive and the
interpretative task in clear focus. Both were convinced that the
Bible contained revelation which could be grasped in the form
of eternal truth neither contaminated nor conditioned by historical limitations. Orthodox interpreters found this revelation in
the whole of Scripture and systematized it by means of a process
of harmonization, interpreting the more difficult passages by
those which fitted hand-in-glove with their own systems. The
liberals arrived at "pure revelation" by way of more or less
drastic reductions decided upon by means of critical methodology. Interestingly, once the actual words of the prophets or of
Jesus were established, these words just happened to square
with the ideals of the modern age.

In spite of these shortcomings, the results of biblical studies
began to make increasingly clear the vast distance between
biblical times and thought and contemporary patterns. In general, biblical theology has responded by accepting the experience
of the strangeness and distance of biblical thought as a creative
asset rather than as a burdensome liability. Regardless of the
judgments we make of their conclusions, such men as Barth,
Bultmann, Cullmann, Wright, von Rad, and Eichrodt have not
been afraid of trying to deal with the horizontal gap between
the revelation events located in the past and the existential needs
of contemporary man. Their efforts can provide stimulus and

substance for the church, as it seeks to communicate the Christ-event in all its wholeness of reality and meaning to the world today.

By concentrating on its descriptive role, biblical scholarship has fostered new interest and new developments in the field of hermeneutics, which have, in turn, resulted in increased interest in the field of biblical studies. For example, Bultmann's plea for demythologizing the New Testament makes it more imperative to have the "original" spelled out in its own terms with the highest degree of perception.

In the Old Testament the descriptive task is constantly affected by the problem of layers of meaning. Any descriptive statement has to be prefaced by the question: "For whom and at what state of Israelite or Jewish history?" The main track along which the biblical theologian pursues the meaning of the Old Testament is that of the ongoing religious life of Israel as the chosen people of God responding to the events in its history which they interpret as the acts of God. In New Testament studies the distinction between the descriptive and interpretive task has not been so clearly maintained. Schweitzer's *The Quest of the Historical Jesus* was a descriptive effort and included only a cautious attempt in an epilogue to draw out the implications of the thorough-going eschatology of Jesus for theology and for life. But Barth and Bultmann were primarily concerned with the present meaning and so lost enthusiasm, the former implicitly, the latter explicitly, for the descriptive task.

Biblical theology has recognized its first task as descriptive, defining the original in its own terms. This has not resulted in the disintegration of the biblical text into unrelated bits of antiquated information, as might have been expected. Working within the restrictions of seeking the answer to the question "What did it mean?" biblical theology is quite capable of viewing the different elements of Scripture as parts of an organic unity. Of course there are limitations. We can treat the Bible as a unity in the sense of interpreting the Old Testament through the lens of the New. This is beyond the descriptive task and involves interpretation based on hermeneutical principles. We can also examine concepts or ideas as they develop through the Bible. One can place himself at the end of the New Testament canon and ask; "How does it all look?" This is clearly within the descriptive task of biblical theology. The sense of biblical unity gained from descriptive studies derives from the unity to which the two Testaments witness when they both are seen as part of a continuing interpreted history.

From this vantage point the Old Testament is seen as the living and growing tradition of a people ever engaged anew in reflecting upon the traditions of its history in the light of new experiences and self-understanding. This "sacred history" continues into the New Testament. Israel's consciousness of God's election is transferred to and received in a heightened sense by the Christians. History is still the matrix of theology. As Israel lives through its history as a chosen people, so the Christians gather together as the chosen ones. The unity of the Bible rests on this historical basis.

This view of the unity of the Bible suggests an approach to the hermeneutical question. If the historical framework of biblical thought is maintained, the bridge between the centuries of biblical events and our own time can be found in the actual history of the church as the ongoing sacred history of God's people. Instead of a God who acted in biblical times but does not act any more, we have a God who still acts in history when he leads his church to new lands and new cultures, new areas of concern, and new forms of ministry. The church is something far beyond an organization for the promotion of theology and evangelism based on a sacred history which ended sometime in the past. Through ongoing sacred history, which is commonly labeled "church history," the fruits of God's acts in covenant and in the Christ are handed down to the present time.

Such an approach raises the problem of the canon in its sharpest form. Judaism, in the time of Jesus, lived under the conviction that the Spirit had withdrawn from the world; thus Israel depended for guidance upon the scriptural interpretation of scribes whose authority rested on faithful transmission. The closing of the New Testament canon did not rest upon such an assumption. The church recognized the continuing work of the Spirit in its life. It also felt the need for a distinction between this activity and the significance of Jesus Christ and his apostles as the "once for all" upon which the church was built. In the canon the church affirms the acts of God in Christ and his apostles as unique, but it also points toward an ongoing history of the church as a valid source of divine guidance.

This historical view gives a new breadth and freedom to the hermeneutical endeavor. The history of Christian theology points to the fact that many philosophies, epistemologies, anthropologies, and the like, may well furnish the framework for a systematic theology by which the contemporary meaning of the Christian Scriptures can be stated. The ongoing work of the Spirit in the history of the church gives us the right to attempt new statements. The efforts of descriptive biblical theology to discern "what is meant" provide the essential foundation and safeguard for such translational activity.

To ask the question: "What does the Scripture mean here and now?" brings us face to face with the hermeneutical problem. Hermeneutics includes the whole task of the exegesis, interpretation, and reinterpretation of the historic documents of the church, particularly the Bible. With the development of literary and historical criticism, however, hermeneutics tended toward a formal literary discipline, more and more separated from the life and proclamation of the Christian community.

Barth's *Romans* marked the beginning of a new approach to hermeneutics. Here hermeneutics became not a theory about interpretation but rather *hermeneia*—a commentary in which the subject matter of Paul's language was radically translated and proclaimed anew in contemporary language. From this beginning has developed the approach known as "the new hermeneutic."

The emphasis of the new hermeneutic is on meaning rather than on interpretation, although interpretation is seen as a necessary step in the process. Hermeneutics seeks to get to the *experience* which gave rise to the text and to state in contemporary language not the text itself but the meaning to which the text witnesses as it addresses man today. Such an effort recognizes that a word is not a statement of what a man says; it is a search for what he *wants* to say. Or, to use Ebeling's idea, the human word is a search for what the word of God wants to say. Hermeneutics attempts to let the word speak that same word today.

When men direct their energies to interpreting the biblical text, the text comes to interpret man. The text becomes the subject of interpretation, rather than simply remaining an object to be interpreted. The text is there not for its own sake but for the sake of the word-event that is both the origin and the future of the text. Word-event includes interpretation which takes place through the word; the text is there for the sake of the event of interpretation. The word that once occurred, and in occurring became the text, must become interpreting word with the help of the text.

The goal of hermeneutics, then, is not simply better understanding, but rather proclamation—a happening of the word-event which calls the hearer to existential faith. The new hermeneutic emphasizes the ultimate and decisive existence of the hearer of the proclamation. The text, rather than being the object of interpretation, becomes an aid in the interpretation of present existence. In order that this may occur, historical research, employing all the tools of that difficult trade, must be vigorously pursued. This research understands itself as subserving the final task of proclamation.

Such developments clearly reflect the emergence of hermeneutics from a subordinate position as a subdivision of biblical studies to a focal theological position. Because the new hermeneutic proposes to bridge the gulf between historical and systematic theology in terms of a recurrent even of language, moving from Jesus' word to that of the preacher, the new hermeneutic presents a new way of looking at theological scholarship as a whole. This overarching implication moving far beyond hermeneutic's function as a subdivision within biblical scholarship becomes most apparent in the work of Ebeling.

Ebeling transforms the translational task of hermeneutics into a total theological enterprise. He revives Bonhoeffer's call for a "non-religious interpretation of biblical concepts" suitable for a "world come-of-age." In this way Ebeling develops a hermeneutic which embraces the doctrine of the word of God and becomes the focus for a total theological position. The new hermeneutic is as much a new theology as were dialectic theology and Ritschlianism. It is Ebeling's conviction that theology *is* hermeneutic, for it consists of translating the Bible into the word for today.

The new hermeneutic deals not only with the interpretation of biblical documents, but also, as a theological position, with the reinterpretation of prior theological formulations, invoking the same principle applied in biblical reinterpretation, namely, that it is not the text itself which is to be interpreted but the intention or experience which gave rise to the text. Although both Ernst Fuchs and Gerhard Ebeling, the two chief exponents of the new hermeneutic, refuse to be characterized as existentialist philosophers, their work is greatly influenced by this philosophy. Both are deeply concerned about "being" and "authentic existence." Language is considered to be a vehicle by which one is brought to "being"; hence the central role given to the "language-event" (Fuchs) or the "word-event" (Ebeling). Hence also the emphasis on faith, which is thought of as man's response to the encounter with God in a multidimensional context.

Since existential theology has not been particularly influential among American theologians, it is difficult at this time to see how the new hermeneutic will be developed in American theology.

It is almost certain to be influential, since there is basic agreement in contemporary theology that the problems of meaningful interpretation and of method are dependent on the realities experienced and known. One major criticism by American theologians is that the existentialist position is essentially subjective and fails to give adequate attention to the importance of cultural factors.

Dillenberger, for example, has noted that the problem for theology here is that its basic formulations have been expressed in a universe of discourse that has been challenged and virtually destroyed by thought processes that have become dominant in the past two centuries. The transition to the modern world includes a fundamental shift from the notion that truth has occurred in the past and is to be uncovered or recovered to the view that truth is to be discovered, that it lies in the future. To Dillenberger this means that God's revealing presence must be thought of in the categories of our own world, even if these categories stand against former categories. The dominant note is openness to the future rather than determination by the past. The truth of God comes to us in our own historic situation. This does not mean that the truth of one period is as good as another nor that all truth is relative. It does mean that the truth of God is only known to us concretely in the forms of the world in which we live.

Braaten also challenges the validity of the existential approach to the hermeneutical problem. He notes that although the existentialist recognizes the fact that every historian approaches the past with his own preunderstandings, existentialism provides a too narrow concept of the preunderstanding that is appropriate to biblical interpretation. Contra Bultmann, such preunderstanding is not given with human existence as such, but is always conditioned by the understanding of faith provided in the community of believers. And such a preunderstanding is certainly not identical in every interpreter of the Bible. There is the reality of a theological dimension that presupposes the hearing of the word within a context of the church and the personal insight of faith.

Braaten stakes out a claim for dogmatics as an essential element in hermeneutics through its power to disclose assumptions at work in biblical interpretation which interpret the text within a too-narrowly preconceived framework. The hermeneutical problem, in his estimation, must be placed within a larger framework that includes the tradition of the church as well as its dogma and liturgy. He feels that the critical-historical method and existentialist (or linguistic) philosophy have recently taken command of hermeneutical efforts. History and tradition, links of the hermeneutical chain that keep us in living contact with the biblical events, have dropped out of sight. A hermeneutic of the word and the church must go beyond the individualism of existentialism to corporate structures, such as dogma and liturgy, which carry the meaning of redemption to God's people through the changing times and situations.

Since the hermeneutical problem focuses upon the meaning of the biblical text for contemporary man, it will inevitably affect the work of every unit within the structure of the church. Modern man, whether conceived of as the national confronted by the Bible teacher in India or Africa, the urban or suburban dweller in America, the theological student, the sophisticated scientist, or the developing child, asks essentially the same question: "What does the word of God mean to me in this present time and place?" As we seek to help him formulate that meaning in teaching and worship materials, the presuppositions of existentialism may prove to be inadequate. But we can still ask the same questions about the nature of human existence and utilize the approaches and findings of the new hermeneutics.

Seemingly, at this point, the most fruitful direction lies in a less subjective and more historical orientation toward both the basic questions and the substance in which we seek answers. Even the structures developed by the church for proclaiming and embodying the word must come under our scrutiny, since one element stressed in the current hermeneutical endeavor points clearly toward the continuing activity and presence of God in the ongoing history of his people and in their interpretation of their message and mission.

## II. CURRENT TRENDS IN
## OLD TESTAMENT INTERPRETATION

In the current stream of biblical studies Old Testament interpretation has assumed growing importance. The church has always had difficulty with the Old Testament. As far back as the second century, Marcion tried to prove that the Old Testament contradicted the New and encouraged Christianity to sever itself from its Old Testament past. The church's response was simply to weld the two testaments together in a doctrinal system that created an uncritical harmonization through the use of allegorical exegesis. Rather than rejecting the Old Testament in toto, it read into it everything that it had learned from the New Testament. The result was that the particular message of the Old Testament was completely lost as if the Old Testament itself had been separated from the Christian canon.

The Old Testament was attacked again after the rise of modern historical criticism. Harnack asked the church to acknowledge that the Old Testament formed no essential part of its faith and life. The church was asked to follow Schleiermacher's recommendation to let the New Testament stand by itself. In Schleiermacher's view, the Old Testament did not share the same normative status as the New. Nor did it evidence for him the same degree of inspiration. Even today existentialist hermeneutical theology, though it does not call for the radical excising of the Old Testament from the canon, looks upon the Old Testament as merely prolegomena to the Christian faith. It may be a revelation of the preunderstanding of faith, that is, of man under the law (of "inauthentic existence"). Unlike the New Testament, it is not a vehicle of God's living word to the church and mankind today.

The two groups of persons so interpreting the Old Testament are the New Testament scholars who have taken their cue from Rudolph Bultmann and systematic theologians who have allowed Luther's dialectic of law and gospel to break the Bible into two pieces, the law representing the Old Testament, and the gospel the New. Braaten believes that modern existentialist theology, as relevant as its insights have been into the nature of human existence, has fallen short in its treatment of the Old Testament, whereas systematic theologians grossly misunderstand Luther's dialectic of law and gospel when they accept it as a basis for separating the two Testaments. Luther maintained that this dialectic of law and gospel does not occur merely between the two Testaments but also within each of them. Even in the Old Testament Israel's interpretation of her own history includes the themes of God's love and grace.

Many voices have protested the traditional schemes of interpreting the Old Testament. One of the most hopeful signs in Old Testament study today is the willingness of scholars to let the Old Testament speak for itself before they ask the question: "What does it all mean for us today?"

James M. Robinson has noted that each generation has elevated a particular theological discipline to a crucial level, primarily because of the impact it has had on cultural environment. He substantiates his point of view by showing that Harnack made church history such a discipline before World War I; Karl Barth made dogmatics the center of concern after World War I; and since World War II, Rudolph Bultmann has won first place for New Testament research. Robinson now suggests that it is quite possible that Old Testament scholarship could move beyond its departmental confines into such a central theological position in our generation. The response to Gerhard von Rad's *Theology of the Old Testament* may be a sign of such a development.

Von Rad has pointed out two very different versions of Israel's history. First, there is the picture that Israel herself has drawn of her own history, her confessional description of her own origins and experiences. Here history is to be seen as a history of God's redemptive actions. Second, there is the picture of Israel's history drawn by modern historiographers who rigorously apply the methods of historical science. The question is, acknowledging these two histories to be a fact, which version should be normative for the church in its proclamation today? Von Rad maintains that we cannot dispense with either one; the theologian must be primarily concerned with the history as Israel remembered it and passed it on and must not substitute for it the current reconstruction.

Two groups of scholars have made proposals on how to resolve the dualism implied in von Rad's position. Exponents of the group sharply opposed to von Rad are Franz Hesse and Frederick Baumgartel. Hesse says that if we must choose between the kerygma and the historical reality, we must choose against the kerygma, because Israel's kerygma was based on events that never happened. Baumgartel would hold that neither of the two versions of history possesses theological relevance; the Old Testament really speaks to us out of a non-Christian religious context and has value only as history of religion or history of piety. Since it is outside of the gospel, it cannot be understood as a series of historical events in which God's will and word were operative.

However, a group of scholars trained under von Rad have proposed a way of reconciling the two versions of history. In New Testament studies this group refused to choose between the historical and the kerygmatic and instead emphasized the mutuality of the two. The historical facts are so welded together with their inherent meanings in the narratives which Israel transmitted that there is no sharp antithesis between fact and interpretation. For these men the key for reconciling the two versions of history is the concept of *tradition* history or *transmission* history. By this they mean the study of the dynamic historical process by which Israel transmitted her creedal testimonies to the acts of God from one generation to the next. This concept is obviously applicable not only to Old Testament scholarship but to the traditions of the primitive Christian church.

One of the most serious difficulties facing Old Testament scholars derives from the fact that not only is the Old Testament composed of historical reports colored by kerygmatic and liturgical influences, but also that the various traditions within the Old Testament contain a variety of theological viewpoints. This situation raises several questions. Given such a variety of materials, how can there be a theology of the Old Testament? Is there any unity or continuing connection among the various reflections on the great moments in Israel's history? Did God act only from time to time and leave Israel to her own devices in the intervening years?

The Pannenberg school suggests one solution. It holds that there are patterns of meaning discernible in the various layers of tradition. There is a rhythm between promises and fulfillments that can be traced in the course of Israel's experience and understanding of her history. A single historical episode could provide several different theological interpretations; as Israel encountered new situations, she interpreted the meaning of the original event in new ways. In this sense the whole history of Israel possesses a continuity even in the discontinuity of times and situations. The entire history, including the history of transmitting and interpreting the redemptive events, is the act of God. God's act cannot be confined to either the single historical events themselves or to the way his people interpret them. Historical reality consists of both dimensions, the outer dimension of observable factual events and the inner dimension of understanding the inherent meaning of the events. The inner dimension is itself an historical event which has a history.

The theological question of the relation of the Old Testament to the New is a central concern of those involved in the current hermeneutical debate. Even though much scholarly work has been done in archeology, literary analysis, form criticism, historical research, and the development of tradition, all of this information must be gathered, examined, and evaluated from the perspective of what is specifically valid and relevant to the existential concerns of faith, of preaching, and of church instruction. There are four lines along which this discussion is moving.

## A. *The Christological Interpretation*

Karl Barth and Wilhelm Vischer have interpreted the Old Testament as a witness to Jesus Christ. They maintain that the revelation in the Old Testament is valid for the church because in these writings Jesus Christ is manifest as the Expected One. They hold that only the church can read the Old Testament rightly because it reads it as the New Testament sees it—as the witness to the coming of Christ. In the Old Testament Jesus is the object of expectation, and in the New, the object of recollection. Barth and Vischer treat the Old Testament as a full partner with the New Testament in the Christian canon. Such an approach to the Old Testament requires us to take seriously the exegetic problem of showing how the role of the Messiah is fulfilled by Jesus.

The Christological approach has its limitations. Not every text in the Old Testament contains Christological content and therefore cannot be interpreted by applying only Christological criteria. An allegorical type of exegesis, which finds depths of meaning in the text that the original authors never imagined, would be invalid. Any effort to maintain the unity existing between the Testaments must avoid the total merging of the two. A wholly Christological interpretation of the Old Testament could ultimately lead to reducing God to Christ and open up the possibility of a Christocentric gnosticism.

## B. *The Existentialist Interpretation*

Rudolph Bultmann has made a strong case for interpreting the Old Testament as a witness to human existence under the law. Bultmann rejects the traditional view of the Old Testament as a book of prophecies that are fulfilled in the New Testament.

He maintains that the New Testament identified prophecies of the Old Testament by reading from present to past, fulfillment to prophecy, rather than from past to present, prophecy to fulfillment. The motive for doing this was polemical in relation to the Jews and apologetic with respect to the Gentiles. Bultmann maintains that, so used, the Old Testament strengthened the arguments for the truth of the salvation-event in Christ. But these arguments represent only attempts to gain security for faith. As such, they subtract from the offense of the Cross, which faith has to overcome in its own way apart from objective proofs. Faith, as Bultmann interprets it, has no place for historical evidences that Jesus Christ is the goal of the prophetic history of Israel.

In dealing with the concepts of covenant, the kingdom of God, and the people of God in the Old Testament, Bultmann concludes that each contains an internal contradiction which prevents its realization within history. As a covenant people under God's rule, Israel conceived of herself as a real historical entity. In the New Testament, however, these concepts are radically eschatologized. For Bultmann the New Testament community is not an historical entity within the world, but rather a dimension outside the world. As such it does not exist as a people requiring an institutional ordinance for its organization. In taking this position, Bultmann destroys any sense of revelational continuity between the history of God's people in the Old Testament and the new people of God in the New Testament.

Bultmann also finds only negative meaning in the Old Testament. He calls it "a miscarriage of history" that can be treated as law because the law reveals man's contradictions and drives him to Christ. It is in this sense of being a revelation of Israel's failure that the Old Testament may be considered a preparation for the gospel. Bultmann, of course, claims the authority of Paul and Luther for bracketing the Old Testament as law. The question, however, is whether the law-gospel dialectic is the sole valid hermeneutic of the Old Testament. It appears that both

Paul and Luther recognized that there is more than law in the Old and grace in the New. The law which the gospel presupposes is not exclusively in the Old Testament. Actually, the demands of the law are universally present and operative in human existence. We may use the Old Testament today as a mirror of our existence under the law, but the church also reads the Old Testament as its own history and as God's word of revelation.

## C. *The Typological Interpretation*

Gerhard von Rad and others established the continuity between the Old and New Testaments by the use of the typological method. The typological way of thinking seeks to discover a corresponding relationship between certain types of the Old Testament, such as persons, institutions, or events, and similar realities or anti-types in the New Testament. Typology must be distinguished from allegory. The difference lies in the greater historical sense of the typologic way of thinking.

Because typology might become overly concerned with insignificant details of correspondence between the two Testaments, von Rad gives typology a clear Christological focus. The premise on which the typological method rests is that the same God who acted in Christ left his footprints in the history of the Old Testament covenant people. Pannenberg maintains, however, that the typological method of exegesis is not sufficient for handling the Old Testament. It is not enough to establish structural agreements between the Christ-event and the Old Testament. These analogies do exist, but their validity rests upon the one history worked out by God which includes both testaments.

## D. *The Historical Interpretation*

The German word *Heilsgeschichte* is generally used to denote that peculiarly biblical view according to which history is tied to the continuing redemptive activity of God. It was with this view in mind that von Rad calls the Old Testament a history book, that is, a record of a series of events directed by the word of God wherein we can discern a full pattern of mutually corresponding prophetic promises and divine fulfillments. Von Rad himself recognizes the danger of a one-sided kerygmatic interpretation of the Old Testament which searches for meanings apart from their rootedness in historical events. The Old Testament is a history not only of the faith of Israel, but also of the activity of God in the earthly experiences of the Hebrew people.

Von Rad's promise/fulfillment scheme has been adopted by Pannenberg and others as a way of bringing the two Testaments together within a historical framework. Walter Zimmerli has observed that "when we survey the entire Old Testament, we find a great movement from promise toward fulfillment. It is like a large brook—here rushing swiftly, there apparently coming to rest in a quiet pool, yet ever moving forward toward a distant goal."

In reviewing each of these approaches, one is led to the judgment that none can claim a monopoly on being *the* hermeneutical avenue into the Old Testament. Each must be evaluated and used in the light of its peculiar strengths and limitations. The Christological approach can clarify the focus of both testaments in Christ if we refrain from using it to the point of an incipient Christocentric gnosticism. The existentialist interpretation can contribute to faith and preaching by its probing of the Old Testament for insights into the nature of man and his existence. But without historical underpinning it becomes little more than religious anthropology. The typological method can direct the search for and the uncovering of genuine correspondence between the two testaments. But to achieve this important goal, it must not be allowed to degenerate into mere allegory. Conceivably the promise/fulfillment scheme offers the best overall way of grasping the indispensable role of the Old Testament for Christian faith and for relating it to the New. But lacking the corrective of the others, it can become formalistic and abstract, tending toward a religious philosophy of history.

Trends in Old Testament studies will have a far-ranging effect on both the self-understanding of the church in its continuing search for identity and in its interpretation and proclamation of the word of God. Current efforts to clarify the task and message of the church in contemporary society are closely tied to a new appreciation of its identification with the Old Testament servant-people of God, of the strong prophetic quality of much of the Old Testament, and perhaps above all, of the doctrine of creation, rooted in the Old Testament. We can expect current lines of emphasis to continue, thus calling for an even larger role for the Old Testament in both the didactic and service areas of church life. Old Testament studies will also play a significant part in interfaith dialogue.

### III. SOME CURRENT EMPHASES IN NEW TESTAMENT INTERPRETATION

For the past quarter century interest in New Testament interpretation has revolved mainly around the demythologization debate brought on by the appearance of Bultmann's essay "New Testament and Mythology" in 1941. Even then the problem of what to do with the mythological elements in the New Testament was not a new one. It has confronted biblical exegetes from the day the worldview taken for granted in the New Testament documents began to change. Liberal theology sought to resolve the problem by eliminating all myth from the New Testament. When this did not work, the problem cried more persistently for attention. As Bartsch has noted, scholars realized that what was needed was "not elimination, but interpretation." In the succeeding years the relation between kerygma and myth became a central concern of New Testament exegesis.

These developments point up sharply one of the two realities in the continuing revolution in which contemporary scholars find themselves as they approach the study of the New Testament records. Such work must be done in full recognition of the historical-critical studies which have become ever more precise and complex and which have completely changed the patterns of biblical studies, presenting us with a variety of techniques and trends that continue to expand. The second important fact in the current situation is the ecumenical movement. Protestant and Catholic scholars no longer live apart, each in separate worlds. Roman Catholics are increasingly using the tools and methods developed by Protestant scholars. The result is that the separate biblical camps are not always related to confessional allegiances. Increasingly one finds in each camp a variety of confessional stances. John Reumann has pinpointed several features of current New Testament scholarship that serve well as points around which to arrange related items.

## A. *The Use of Scientific Methods of Bible Scholarship*

Nineteenth-century Protestantism, particularly in Germany, made the decision to apply the historical-critical method to Bible study, come what may. The decision can be viewed as having as great a significance as the sixteenth-century reformers' endorsement of "grace and faith alone." In the past century critical methods have been applied, refined, and expanded. Today Roman Catholic scholars as well as Protestant (including some conservatives), having tasted the liberation achieved through historical-critical techniques, see no possibility of a return to the precritical era. This means that not merely textual, literary, and source criticism are here to stay. To them must be added form and editorial criticism and the history of the transmission of biblical materials. An additional element is a history-of-religions approach, which looks at biblical elements of Christianity in the light of the total history of religion.

What this means specifically as we apply it to New Testament studies will become more apparent in the paragraphs that follow. Some attention will need to be given, however, to the implications inherent in the more radical and extensive use of the historical-critical method of Bible study promised for the future.

Currently the Lutheran Church in America has a large constituency which has accepted the principle of biblical criticism intellectually but certainly not viscerally or emotionally. To anticipate not a less but an even more thorough use of biblical criticism in New Testament studies may appear to many to be a threat to the core of the Christian faith.

## B. *The Rapid Pace of Change in New Testament Studies*

The revolution in New Testament studies is moving so rapidly that what is announced confidently as the tested fruit of scholarship may already be considered dubious or passé by the time it is widely disseminated. The whole field is in a state of flux. Examples may be seen in the questioning of the idea that Jesus himself combined the notion of Isaiah's "Suffering Servant" with Daniel's "Son of man" in his own self-awareness; the growing doubts about the relevance and glowing future forecast for the "new hermeneutics"; and the faltering of the "new quest" for the historical Jesus.

The original quest grew out of the introduction of eighteenth-century critical methods of biblical study. It was motivated in general by the widespread interest in the historical study of the Bible, but particularly by the desire to "free Christianity from the Church's teaching about Jesus." It was an effort to get back to "Jesus as he actually was" before he had been obscured by the church's dogmas about him. Schweitzer pointed out that pictures of Jesus produced by earlier historical scholarship were not historical in the scientific sense; each scholar had given the historical figure new life by reading into him the ideas of the scholar's own time. But Schweitzer's own thoroughgoing historical study, *The Quest of the Historical Jesus*, resulted in a Jesus who receded into the past of a Jewish apocalypticism utterly alien to contemporary thought patterns and times.

Following Schweitzer, the quest of the historical Jesus largely came to an end as basic shifts in New Testament scholarship seemed to indicate both the impossibility and illegitimacy of such a search. The quest was considered impossible because of the lack of basic and necessary data. It was considered illegitimate on grounds of existential theology. The Gospels were viewed not as history, but kerygma. The central content of the kerygma is God's eschatological action in the cross and resurrection—an event which recurs in the preaching of the kerygma which calls each hearer to accept his own death and resurrected life. Attempts to insure faith by using scientific scholarship to reconstruct a historical Christ are equivalent to an attempt to prove faith, and ultimately amount to a denial of the legitimacy of faith which borders on unbelief.

The new quest differs from the old in that it does not seek to prepare a carefully documented life of Jesus. On the one hand, it is based on the recognition that the historical study of the Gospels did not end with the first quest; today we seem to have far more reliable information than was previously recognized. On the other hand, the primary stimulus for the new quest derives from the question of continuity between the intention and selfhood of the historical Jesus and the proclamation of the church. Is the proclamation of the exalted Lord in the kerygma in some kind of identifiable continuity with the preaching of the historical Jesus? Thus the purpose of the new quest has been to test whether the kerygmatic understanding of Jesus' existence corresponds to the understanding of experience implicit in Jesus' history as analyzed by modern historiography. It is felt that the documents provide sufficient evidence to make a historical encounter with Jesus possible. His actions, his intentions, the understanding of existence they imply, and thus his selfhood, can be identified historically. And this can in turn be compared with the kerygmatic message of the Gospels.

What has come of this effort? Apparently it is already becoming fragmented and is moving in several different directions. Bornkamm's *Jesus of Nazareth*, a major product of the new quest, can be viewed as an optimistic version of Bultmann's *Jesus and the Word*. Other scholars included in the new quest have attempted to find links between the Jesus of history and the kerygma of the early church by emphasizing a concept of human existence common to both, to find a Christology implicit in Jesus' ministry (which becomes explicit after Easter), or to find Jesus' faith in God as the element of continuity with the church's faith in the Risen One. The new quest has at times reverted to psychologizing about Jesus or searching for his "very voice" if not his very words. In spite of these many efforts, solid facts about the historical Jesus are as uncertain in many ways as ever.

## C. *Diversity in Current New Testament Interpretation*

The history of New Testament interpretation, like Old Testament study, has witnessed alternating emphases on the unity and diversity of the New Testament writings. Pietism regarded them as materials which could be ordered under a series of neatly arranged headings, all pointing to a basic unity. The dogmatic orthodoxists tried to weld the teachings of the New Testament into a harmonious system to which one could turn in time of crisis and deduce a doctrine or position to meet the current problem. What the New Testament writers had to say was funneled through an organizing principle, such as justification by grace through faith or a theology of the cross (a "canon within a canon").

Presently there is a growing feeling that such efforts not only strain out the richness of the biblical witness but also do violence to its essential character. We shall need to recognize that there never existed any sort of monolithic orthodoxy among the New Testament writers. Each evangelist had his own theology. In a recently published study of Luke, Helmut Flender points out that the distinctiveness of Lucan theology has become increasingly apparent during the past few years. Luke does not merely transmit the tradition as it came to him; he is a theologian interpreting the Christian message for his own time. His interpretation is guided by theological presuppositions which identify him as a theologian of the post-apostolic age. The received tradition is modified by being placed in a given dogmatic framework. Concentration on contemporary theological witness is accompanied by an attrition of the tradition. The contemporary dogmatic scheme determines and alters the meaning of the traditional terms. That leads to the "promiscuous" use of Christological titles. Luke uses them in a way which is quite different from the meaning they originally intended.

The necessity of no longer talking of a theology of the New Testament, but of its theologies, has a number of implications. For one, we recognize even in the New Testament that the idea of *Heilsgeschichte* is simply a theological construct found in varying degrees among certain biblical writers and their interpreters. This is not to deny that some biblical authors utilize a *heilsgeschichtlich* view, whereby history is divided into a sequence of periods in which God is understood to have acted to work salvation. It is simply to recognize that such theories are retrospective, that they look back over past history from a given theological vantage point, that they make use of certain assumptions, and that they vary from author to author.

Along the same line of thought we find that there are a number of "salvation histories," both in the Old and New Testaments, among which there is not always common agreement. Mark, Matthew, and Luke each has a distinct view of salvation and history. In Mark this comes to a focus on Jesus' struggle with Satan for power in history, so that Jesus is seen as primarily preaching not the coming of the kingdom but the calling of the disciples (the church) to participate in his own eschatological struggle with Satan. On the other hand, Matthew underscores Jesus' role as the Messianic righteous teacher. In Matthew, Christology, ecclesiology, and eschatology are bound together by this concept.

The stress on diversity makes us painfully aware that the New Testament writings are addressed to specific situations which existed in the life of the church at the time they were written.

We dare not use them to find the answers to all of our theological and life problems. Some true analogies can be drawn between past and present, but we may have to use the New Testament more as a critique or prompting than a source of primary datum.

## D. *The Importance of the Eschatological*

The epochal work of Johannes Weiss and Albert Schweitzer at the turn of the century brought into sharp focus the dominance of eschatology in the teachings of Jesus and the early church. It had two consequences. It destroyed the foundations of liberal theology by pointing out that the kingdom of God consisted of an act of renewal, a breaking in from above, brought about by God, and not a cooperative project worked out between God and man. It also pointed out that eschatology deals not only with "last things" in the chronological sense, but "ultimate things" in the existential sense.

The rediscovery of eschatology has been handled in a number of ways: sometimes by regarding apocalyptic thought as an irrelevant mistake by Jesus and the early church; sometimes by reaffirming apocalyptic expectations for today or by seeing positive values in apocalyptic (an ever-future aspect to God's promises); sometimes by exegetical reinterpretation of eschatology. Currently there is attention to futurist or apocalyptic eschatology, "an eschatology that is in the process of realization," and of "inaugurated eschatology." It is of the nature of theologians to come down on one or the other of these emphases. However, the eschatology of the New Testament contains elements of both the present and the future, thus disproving any form of wholly realized eschatology.

The new appreciation for New Testament eschatology may derive in part from the current worldview. We do not think of the world as static, but rather as a process which carries within it possibilities for unimaginable achievements and unimaginable disasters. Contemporary man is oriented toward the future and is open to the expectation that the future may be radically different from the present. In searching for the meaning of life, modern man looks not to the past or even to the present, but to what lies ahead. That which transcends the reality which we experience and know is no longer thought of as a realm of timeless truth, value, and being which supplies permanently stable structures of life. Rather, that which transcends the world of our experience lies ahead, in the indecipherable possibilities for good and evil which the future holds. Our contemporaries do not encounter transcendence as something separate from the world, something to be encountered by escaping out of time into eternity. Rather, they meet it as the future which is both continuous with and radically different from our present world. They encounter it within the reality of their experiences as the anticipations or projections of what the future holds. Biblical apocalypticism, even though couched in ancient symbols, may not be so alien to contemporary man as was supposed. It offers a message of hope for a future which will bring the fulfillment of the promises of righteousness for all, the resurrection of all the dead, and the universal acknowledgment of Jesus Christ as Lord.

# 3

# Christian Ethics

## I. DEFINITIONS AND DIMENSIONS

The terms "ethic," "ethics," and "ethical" are used in a variety of ways. On the practical level "ethics" and "ethical" refer to the content of right action or the code which prescribes it. Thus: "Dr. Jones is an ethical practitioner. He never violates professional ethics." On a more abstract level the term "ethic" is used to denote that body of moral attitudes which characterize a culture, subculture, or religious ethos. Hence the Protestant or Puritan ethic or the American business ethic. Finally, "ethics" denotes that intellectual discipline, traditionally considered a subdivision of philosophy or theology, which treats of the norms of human conduct. Thus, ethics may be defined as that discipline having as its proper activity the discovery, criticism, and elucidation of the norms of human conduct. Christian ethics may be defined as that discovery, criticism, and elucidation as it is done within the believing community against the background of revelation, and the response to that revelation which together constitute the community's peculiar history, and in dialogue with the contemporary world. In this chapter, the term "ethics" will be used to denote both the intellectual discipline defined here and the content of particular ethical systems or points of view.

Ethics lies at that vital center, man-in-relationship, where a host of other disciplines converge. In its effort to take account of the social, cultural, and psychological dynamics of human action, ethics employs the language and findings of the behavioral sciences. In its concern to see and evaluate norms in the light of the cumulative experience of the past, it takes on the coloration of historiography. Endeavoring to ground its assertions ontologically, it speaks with the voice of the philosopher and theologian. Finally, as it seeks to explicate the shape and content of man's action in the many areas of his everyday life, ethics employs the speech of a vast number of realms—politics, economics, industrial relations, international diplomacy, and medicine, to name but a few.

Ethics operates within the tension between such elements as freedom and responsibility, grace and law, dynamics and form, individual and community. Like philosophy, it must deal with the tensions between being and becoming and between the universal and the particular. Perhaps more than any other human enterprise. ethics must constantly work between the poles of reflection and action, of the ideal and the actual, of ought and is.

In recent years, particularly in America, ethicists have increasingly emphasized the social or interpersonal nature of their subject matter. Such is the case not only with those whose tradition is of an antinomian coloration (as is the "ethics of inspiration" characteristic of portions of left-wing Protestantism) but also with those whose heritage is in terms of principles, created structures, or natural law. This broadly-based trend contains within it a dialectic which will be discussed presently. Suffice it here to say that, accounting for all degrees and variations, Christian ethics is increasingly taking on the character of what was once a subdivision within it—social ethics. The social sources and consequences of human action are becoming to one degree or another the major interest of all ethical thinkers and not simply of a minority of specialists.

Modern anthropology and psychology emphasize that man realizes who he is only through his relationships with others. Consciousness becomes aware of itself only when it is "intentional"; it is real to itself only when it is related to something else. Even before a child becomes conscious of himself at the beginning of life, he is open to his environment and participates in it. His need for affection, protection, and security creates an emotional symbiosis with his environment. In his deep-set relationship with his mother, the child mimics her look, her gestures, and the sound of her voice. Later, the child comes more and more to understand the meaning of the words he hears, the purpose of the objects he sees, and the reason for the actions he observes.

Congenial with this trend is the description of ethics as the science of responsible personhood. "Personhood" is here understood in terms of dynamic relationships: there are no persons without human communities to which they are related. "Responsible" describes right action as that which is done in answer (response) to the action of other members of the social organism and, ultimately, in answer to the action of God. This formulation, which is essentially that of H. Richard Niebuhr, has not, to be sure, been consciously adopted by all ethicists, but its basis insight—the social character of the self—has wide influence.

It should be noted that this tendency does not represent an uncritical appropriation of the idea of the self as socially determined, a dominant motif in the thought of such men as John Dewey and George Herbert Mead. Certain seminal insights of these men are being carried forward in a form which reflects the influence of existential phenomenology ("I-thou"), of which Martin Buber is a chief representative. The far-reaching character of this tendency is illustrated in the way it is affecting Roman Catholic moral theologians, for instance, Albert Dondeyne, Bernard Haring, and Joseph Pieper.

One may reasonably ask what it is that has occasioned the trend. While it is impossible to isolate all the factors which have caused the trend or contributed to it, it is fairly accurate to say that the human problems accompanying rapid change and growth of mass society have driven ethicists to inquire primarily not about principles and duties, but rather about what it means to be a person in a world where personhood and the relationships which underlie it appear to be increasingly fragmented.

It appears that modern man is simultaneously becoming increasingly more public and more private. Collectively he is becoming increasingly public. Mass media, communication, and the ubiquitous and omniscient computer leave man utterly exposed. The problems of mass society are necessarily of a public nature and demand public political answers. All members of society are involved in these problems and, however passively, in their solutions. All are the beneficiaries or the victims of these solutions. Individually modern man is becoming increasingly private. Overawed by the bigness of corporate society, rendered anxious by its anonymity and cold functionalism, he flees or is driven into his private world. It is here that he seeks to create meaning for himself, to find diversion by means of his affluence. Here he seeks authentic personal relationships or, failing those, some tolerable facsimile.

Given this situation, the urgent question is: How can man become a fully responsible person-in-relationship in the totality of his existence, both private and public? What correctives must be brought to bear in order to keep man from restricting his personhood to the private world while allowing himself to become an ethically neutral cog in the machinery of corporate public life? Put most starkly: How is man to be kept from being utterly rent asunder, privately a St. Francis, publicly an Eichmann? Since the church continues to operate mainly within man's "private sector" even to the point of treating its message as a consumer commodity to be merchandised in the most attractive manner possible, the implications of these questions for its program and life are overwhelming.

## II. CONTEMPORARY APPROACHES IN CHRISTIAN ETHICS

It may be helpful at this point to indicate in a general way a few of the more direct responses that the present situation is evoking.

Such a discussion will more fully set the stage for the later spelling out of fundamental issues. Three examples are offered here: Harvey Cox, Philip Hefner, and Gibson Winter.

One of the most popular and controversial responses is that of Harvey Cox. More a tractarian than a scholar, Cox presented in *The Secular City* what amounts to a celebration of urban anonymity and the technology which produced it as the very masks of the gospel. Through the anonymity and functionalism of urban life man is liberated from the bondage of "town life," a bondage characterized by bogus religiosity and false personal relationships in a "fishbowl" existence. No Huxlian brave new world, "technopolis" is hailed as (potentially at least) the City of God. Urbanization is seen as a liberation from some of the bondages of simpler society. It offers a chance to be free, it delivers man from enforced convention. Being anonymous in most relationships permits urban man to have a face and a name for others. (In more recent publications Cox develops a somewhat different viewpoint.)

Cox's ideal, liberated, urban man seems close to the concept of "therapeutic man" set forth by Philip Rieff. Therapeutic man is the detached, uncommitted individual par excellence. Never attached passionately to any one particular meaning or object, therapeutic man does not need to keep a safe distance from the mass of his fellows. He can be so trained as to minimize vulnerability. To live on the surface prevents deep hurts.

Philip Hefner stands with those opposed to the tendency toward a "privatization" of man. If the church is to contribute to the search for meaning in the midst of cultural revolution, if it is to help clarify what life can be in the post-Christian era, it will have to balance two elements in its own life and message. It will have to tear away the veil that hides the false bias against community commitment and creative renunciation. It will have to acknowledge that its own community and the commitments involved in it will exist under conditions quite different from the past, in forms quite new.

Hefner contends that the church cannot be true to its nature if it allows itself simply to become an agency devoted to helping therapeutic man become ever more skillful in his detachment and uncommitment. Such a course would reduce the church to the status of a counseling clinic helping an already over-privatized, over-individualized man to accept the isolation which accompanies his state in order to more effectively "negotiate" with —but not establish community with—his world. Hefner holds that the church, itself a community, should promote community in the larger world. While welcoming with Rieff, Cox, and others the freedom from false commitments (heteronomies) afforded by the culture of the post-Christian metropolis, Hefner maintains that freedom from false commitments cannot mean freedom from all commitments. "Private" man is a truncated caricature; the new man in Christ is essentially "related," "public" man. Hefner (and those who make a similar emphasis) do not, of course, intend that attention be diverted away from what might be called the meaning and content of selfhood. The private side of personality cannot be neglected; the pathological blockages to a person's *becoming* a neighbor are as important as the public content of *being* a neighbor. The two questions must be held together: How is a man to be freed to be a neighbor? And what is to be the content of being a neighbor in the present world, in both its private and public, its individual and corporate dimensions?

Another thinker unwilling to settle for the image of an essentially privatized man is Gibson Winter. Standing in sharp contrast to writers who seem to make virtue of the breakdown of the community of space (town, neighborhood, parish), Winter calls for a restoration of spatial communities in which there is variety in both residents and activities. The place, in Winter's view, has relevance for Christian ethics as it had, along with time, in the Incarnation.

Basically, Winter's desire is to work toward the healing of human community broken by the specialization of technopolis.

Metropolitan life evidences an expanding, impersonal interdependence and growing exclusiveness in local community groupings. These trends seem to be working at cross-purposes. This double trend is symbolized by the super-highway joining the functional, productive segments of a metropolis while at the same time dividing or even obliterating older neighborhoods. The superhighway leaps over areas of poverty, particularly the racial ghettos, thereby sealing them off still more from participation in the economic mainstream and rendering them for all practical purposes invisible.

Winter points out that the church, in identifying itself with the private residential aspect of life, has unwittingly contributed to this situation of social fragmentation. Indeed, the church has become one of the chief agents in the freezing of patterns of private exclusiveness. The result is an ironic situation in which the avowed champion of reconciliation is a major obstacle to it. This being so, it is in Winter's view doubly incumbent upon the church to make tangible efforts at eliminating those barriers between men which it has itself helped to solidify. His proposal of larger parishes which include a variety of residential and other areas is by now well known. However, his interest goes beyond a restructuring of church life. He also believes that the church must accept as part of its central task active participation in the shaping of social policies which create greater opportunities for contact, exchange, and mutual enrichment among men of varying racial, cultural, and economic backgrounds.

The preceding discussion has attempted to present three responses of Christian ethics to the current social situation in America. Implicit here is the fact that Christian ethicists are all being drawn increasingly into an engagement with the empirical problems of the time—an engagement which is reflected in the manner in which they deal with the basic issues of ethics. It is to some of these basic issues that we now turn.

Altering somewhat the definition given at the beginning of this chapter, Christian ethics may be defined as the critical quest—

in the light of revelation, the cumulative experience of the believing community, and the circumstances and demands of the present-day world—for those elements which constitute right action. It will be noted at once that, in this altered definition, reference to norms does not appear. This change has been made not because the terms "norm," "normative," or "normal" are in themselves illegitimate. Any ethical statement, however qualified, which is intended to say something about "right" action must necessarily be of a normative character. Rather, the definition has been altered to illustrate the increasing shift of emphasis away from a preoccupation with *rigid* norms (whatever their source, whether natural law, biblical positivism, a theory of orders of creation, or some other) and toward concern for right action in the context of a growing understanding of personhood-in-community.

This trend is one which, while hardly new, is now coloring to one degree or another the writing of all Christian ethicists. Gone is the Kantian duty-ethic which influenced much of Protestantism during the nineteenth and early twentieth centuries; going is the rigid conception of natural law that dominated Roman Catholic ethics prior to John XXIII and Vatican II; and gone is the use of the Bible as the source of revealed morality, a use which obtained in both fundamentalism and (in the form of "the teachings of Jesus") liberalism. Christians of all traditions are recovering the essentially biblical insight that man-in-relationship is the proper focus of ethical inquiry.

William R. Rogers makes the point that Christian faith begins with relatedness. Faith is in a person, according to biblical testimony. The relation between God and man is the subject of faith. The relation between man and man is the subject of ethics. These two relationships must not be segregated, since they are complementary throughout the Bible. They are two aspects of a single dynamism in human experience. Joseph Sittler also emphasizes that the vocabulary of relatedness permeates every primary term in the Bible.

This emphasis on the relational character of ethical reflection appears in Paul Lehmann's contextual ethics with its strong emphasis upon the matrix within which ethical action takes place. Even such a term, however, is of an ambiguous character, meaning different things to different ethicists. Lehmann's *Ethics in a Christian Context* uses it to denote the Christian fellowship from which the individual Christian receives his clues as to what "God is doing" in the world. In Lehmann's view, these clues are what assist the Christian to make certain that his own actions in the world coincide with God's "Context" should in no sense be confused or equated with Joseph Fletcher's "situation." The latter assumes the possibility of authentic ethical decision shaped by external circumstances and loses altogether the *simul peccator* and "necessary evil" elements. It emphasizes the situation as shaping action and neglects the possibility of action—and norms —shaping a situation.

For someone operating with the thought framework of H. Richard Niebuhr, context has a meaning considerably more inclusive: the totality of social relationships as well as the transcendent God-relationship that is present in and through them. Still another use of context is that made by Kenneth Underwood to denote the multiplicity of factors which must be known in order to make a responsible decision within a specific sphere of human activity (such as business or government). There are significant criticisms which are being voiced by many who, while they have not themselves gone unaffected by the trend toward relational or contextual thought, are unwilling to go the full distance with such men as Lehmann and Fletcher.

A criticism to which Lehmann is especially vulnerable may be stated as follows: While eschewing ideals or principles as being both dehumanizing and limiting to the freedom of God, Lehmann substitutes an ideal of a different kind, an ideal koinonia. While this ideal church envisaged by Lehmann is of help in judging the shortcomings of the empirical church, it is, like Reinhold Niebuhr's "impossible ethical ideal," quite incapable of achievement in any final form, and its approximations are at best few and far between. With the Protestant sectarians of the past, Lehmann forgets that the church, like its members, is *simul justus, simul peccator* and always *in via.* For that reason, Christians and the church continue to need the law. A koinonia ethic, which is essentially an ethic of inspiration, is at best unreliable.

A second major criticism, generally associated with the name of Paul Ramsey, is that contextualism amounts to an ethic based on the exceptional case. Ramsey understands Christian love to work within and not without rules. Principles act as a safeguard not only against faulty judgment but also against the kind of self-deceiving, facile rationalization which turns freedom into license. Ramsey asserts that, generally speaking, ethical principles are of help to the man who cannot possibly know all the relevant factors when confronted with a decision. Rules normally help in building up personal relationships rather than stifling them, since they protect the individual and the person he confronts against their own worst selves. Ramsey allows for the exceptional case when a rule must be bypassed in order for right action to be performed, but he insists that it is just that, an exception.

The sharp controversy between contextualism and the ethics of "inprincipled love" seems now to be softening considerably. It is generally agreed that supposedly unprincipled ethics do in fact employ principles as ingredients in decision-making and that principled ethics operate situationally. Even Roman Catholic moral theologians, while continuing to espouse natural law, are becoming more personalistic and contextual in their application of it. Protestant ethicists, on the other hand, see the relevance of principles—whether derived from the created structures or from the cumulative experience of the believing community in its engagement with the world.

Gibson Winter's *Elements for a Social Ethic* may well signal the conclusion of this phase of ethical debate and a turning to other issues. Tracing the development of social ethics within the context of the evolution of the social sciences away from dogmatic systems and into a period of phenomenological methodology, Winter comes up with an ethical method which he calls "historical contextualism." This method gathers up into a synthesis those elements which formerly divided ethicists into separate camps. It considers the fitness of the set of conditions, the organization of values, and the set of interests in the light of the emerging needs of human community and personal freedom. In this sense, love as concern for particular beings and concrete situations replaces both legalistic ethics and situational ethics.

This approach takes all the ingredients mentioned above and places them within the dynamic context of man-in-community-in-history. In so doing it gives due weight to principles and values as seen and criticized, in the light of the divine action in Christ and the demands of a given historical moment. Through a process which Winter calls "historical hermeneutics" all the ingredients of ethics are judged in the light of a single principle —divine *agape*. The task of social ethics is to discern the interplay of law, order, and power and to evaluate the relevance of particular norms within historical possibilities. The unification of perspectives by love offers no *a priori* solutions to particular historical problems; it merely ranks the values which can guide decisions. Ethical inspiration is no substitute for historical discernment. Historical discernment without norms is prejudiced by subjective interest and current cultural values.

It is worth noting at this point that some of the directions taken by Winter are also being taken by some Lutheran ethicists. Christian Walther, for instance, writes of the need for intensified attention to social ethics not as a mere "socio-tactical adaptation to contemporary society" but rather as the church performing its proper function of *interpreting* the will of God to man where he is. Walther makes three significant points:

First, the basis for social ethics is the doctrine of creation, understood not in the sense of "orders of creation" but rather in the sense of the early Protestant doctrine of *creatio continua*. This understanding of the process of creation as history gives to the question of the relation of church and society its proper place. Both church and society can be seen as entities involved in God's action in history.

Second, social ethics makes the essentially eschatological affirmation that secular society occurs in the context of the history of God with man that moves toward the consummation of the kingdom of God, a consummation outside man's control. Far from being an uncritically optimistic welcoming of every development as the work of God, theology opens up an aspect which makes it possible to interpret changes in social relationships differently from neo-romantic of conservative representatives of social ethics, who see them as decline. It is not possible to provide a theologically sanctioned optimism of progress which basically knows nothing of sin and grace. It is now possible to accept the present in its relativity and unfinished state as the concrete historical place where discipleship of Christ is to be put to the test.

Third, in this context of *creatio continua* and with an essentially eschatological perspective, Christian ethics is basically a hermeneutical or interpretive activity, a disciplined explication of the word of God received in faith in terms of a "prior examination and analysis of man's being-in-the-world." Such interpretive work must be done carefully and self-critically lest social ethics make a premature peace with the status quo and become the stronghold of social prejudice and resentments.

There now seems to be emerging the beginning of a consensus in which it is more or less agreed that: (1) humanly responsible action is necessarily preceded and followed by rational reflection; (2) ethical decisions, whether by individual persons or by corporate groups, are made against the background of an accumulation of ethical reflection; (3) such cumulative reflection issues in norms or principles; and (4) the work of criticizing and refining these principles is carried out to assist the community and its members to act responsibly, not for the sake of the principles themselves but for the sake of persons.

### III. NEW UNDERSTANDINGS OF TRADITIONAL FORMULATIONS

Not a few of those criticizing contextualism are ethicists concerned about discovering and elucidating basic structures of justice which are not tied to a specifically Christian context. These thinkers find unsatisfactory the Christological or koinonia ethics and consequently are looking for a new relevance in what may be broadly termed natural law. Natural law may be defined as that inherent sense of the right or the just considered to be a part of man's essential humanity. Found in a number of ancient philosophies, natural law received its classic explication from Aristotle. The basic concept of natural law found its way into Christian thought as early as apostolic times when Paul made his well-known reference to the law written on the hearts of men (Romans 1:15). Borrowing from the Aristotelian system, Thomas Aquinas gave natural law its normative statement for Roman Catholics. Non-Roman Christianity has kept elements of the natural law idea.

The discussion of natural law is of course not new. The debate and dissension concerning the correct relationship between nature and grace, law and gospel, justice and love is as old as the church itself. What is new is the current blurring of the old battle lines and the effort by all parties to understand these realities in terms that are more dynamic and flexible.

On the Roman Catholic side there is the tendency to reconceptualize natural law and its relation to love in such a way as to escape the legalistic rigidity of an earlier day. On the Protestant side there is some dissatisfaction with the legacy of Barth and Bonhoeffer in which theology and ethics were reduced to

Christology. On both sides there is a growing interest in creation not as a static "given" but as an ever-new open-ended process.

In Protestant circles the tide of Barthian theology all but swept away interest in or respect for natural theology and its ethical derivative—natural law. The disinterest in and, indeed, contempt for natural theology, natural law, and created orders is seen most sharply in the thought of those "radicals" who, having reduced theology to Christology and Christology to ethics, dismissed investigations into the structures and process of being (creation) with a wave of the hand as having no present significance. The result is a metaphysical nihilism in which such a Christological ethics works itself out into a pragmatism which admits of no philosophical point of reference.

Such a picture would of course be grossly unfair if it did not take account of such critics of natural law as Reinhold Niebuhr —critics who could hardly be classified as metaphysical nihilists. Niebuhr, for instance, never repudiated the capacity of man rationally to apprehend the content of original righteousness. With Brunner, he rejected the Barthian position that the divine image is utterly obliterated by the Fall. Niebuhr's criticism of natural law was rather a criticism of the rational optimism inherent in the traditional Catholic understanding. He insisted on the essential unity of the self and consequently on the distortive and corruptive effect of sin upon the entire self, including its rational function. Niebuhr was a realist regarding the corruptibility of human reason in its quest for justice, but he maintained, nevertheless, that an "inchoate sense" of the absolute demand of justice continues to reside in sinful man.

Unfortunately, this incisive and balanced critique of natural law was all but forgotten by a generation of theologians overwhelmed by the fragmented legacy of Bonhoeffer. Only now are some of them fully awakening to the cul-de-sac into which the pragmatic extremism and metaphysical nihilism of the post-Barthian radicals eventually leads.

The unacceptability of such a reductionism is giving rise to a renewed interest in natural theology and a reappreciation of the classical formulations of natural law (Aristotle, Thomas Aquinas), orders of creation and civil righteousness (the Lutheran Reformers and Lutheran orthodoxy). Such reappreciation, however, is not to be thought of as simple repristination. In this recovery the structures of creation are no longer seen as having the fixity which was once attributed to them. The sciences, particularly the natural sciences, have disallowed such rigidity, thus requiring structures to be seen as embodying a dynamic organic relatedness. Where form once dominated, form and dynamic are now to be held together in tension.

Michael Novak offers a striking example of how far the current restatement of natural law theory can go in Roman Catholicism. Rejecting the traditional notion of natural law as having an independent, hypostatic reality, Novak (along with such men as Dom Odom Lottin and Bernard Lonergan) contends that there are unchanging principles of natural law only in the sense in which operations of intelligence are principles, not in the sense of propositions, precepts, or premises. The operations of intelligence are: experience that raises questions, inquiry that leads to insight, further inquiry testing insights against evidence, and decisions whether or not to act according to experience, insight, and evidence. Novak is obviously open to the criticism that he has for all practical purposes done away with natural law while keeping the term. Yet his effort at retaining what to him is the basic insight of the tradition, human rationality in search of justice, is a significant instance of what is being attempted through the community of Roman Catholic ethicists.

The preceding discussion has been illustrative of how Roman Catholic moral theologians are seeking to reappropriate the idea of natural justice (in contradistinction to a Christological ethic) in a dynamic organic manner which is in keeping with the demands of the present. A similar effort is being carried on by Lutherans, and it is to this that we now turn.

What the Lutheran Reformers sought to do in declericalizing

the secular or, in the words of William H. Lazareth, in "putting the state back under God's law," has continuing relevance today. The work of reaffirming the under-God holiness of the secular against those who wish falsely to "sacralize" or "religionize" it appears never to be finished. In its present form, that task is concentrating on a number of new themes.

The increased pluralism which characterizes modern society calls for a more comprehensive theology of society and of social institutions. Such a theology should not, of course, overlook the special responsibilities and powers which constitute civil government, including the "power of the sword," but it should see these in the context of the multiplicity of interacting institutions (organized labor, the business and industrial complex, protest movements, to name but a few) which have a profound bearing on the secular life of man.

The traditional theology of orders with its emphasis upon the state as an abstraction does not deal adequately with government as an everchanging process. Not only is there an increasing pluralism of institutions within society generally, but there is as well an ever-growing pluralism of function within government itself. No longer is it possible, as it was in the Reformation period, to concentrate upon the "police power" of government as a bulwark against wickedness. The ever-expanding activity of government—under the pressure of and in concert with other secular institutions—in pushing out the boundaries of that which is known as "justice," requires modifications of the traditional Lutheran concept of "orders."

As a corollary to the prior assertions, it is concluded that the characteristically Lutheran emphasis on obedience to authority ought to be replaced by an emphasis on participation in the secular process for the sake of justice. Efforts have been made in this direction by such persons as William Lazareth and George Forell. The fact remains, however, that Lutherans in America tend to shy away from political participation, particularly when it takes a quasi-revolutionary character.

Finally, any relevant theology of society or social ethics must deal with government against the background of two ever-present and somewhat contradictory realities. There is, on the one hand, the vital necessity of securing some sort of viable world order, of providing institutional structures (both within and between nations) which make for that stability necessary for the preservation of life and the assurance of its continuation. On the other hand, there is the equally vital necessity of taking seriously those revolutionary movements which seek to establish economic and social justice for masses of men hitherto deprived of it. The present task, then, is a double one: to affirm and identify with revolution without thereby becoming enthralled by anarchy, and to search for viable institutional forms without becoming the slaves of reaction.

It appears that those aspects of Reformation theology which emphasize obedience as the hallmark of good citizenship, interfere with the realization of the original Reformation intent in contemporary society. What is needed is the creative affirmation of "under-God" (or perhaps for today, "in-God") secularity and a meaningful participation in it. The implications of this situation for the church's educational enterprise should be clear. A bold and imaginative program must be developed at all levels—parish, church college, seminary—to encourage the kind of free and creative secular participation called for today. This may mean laboratory situations in which the learner, be he preschooler or theological student, is involved in some essentially political activity designed to secure greater degrees of human justice. The situations of action and risk-taking, such as those in which many Negro children and youth have taken part, ought in some degree to be part of the education of Christians generally.

## IV. SOME CURRENT ISSUES

A fundamental question that needs to be answered by the exponents of various theories of natural law and created orders is: To what extent is natural justice inherent in all men and to what extent is the idea of this natural justice actually a vestige of the *ethos* that obtained under medieval *corpus Christianum*? Or, put another way, in the effort to find a consensus among all "men of good will" as to the content of justice, is there a danger of neglecting the extent to which a specific religious ethos (e.g., Hindu, Moslem, Christian, Marxist) in fact determines what is to be considered as basic justice?

Roman Catholicism is discovering not only the dynamic aspect of justice but also the fact that certain tenets which it had long considered part of natural law are considered by those outside its fellowship, as well as by many within it, sectarian morality. The traditional Roman Catholic attitudes on birth control and abortion are obvious instances. Protestants with a tradition of moral legalism are discovering the same thing. Not only are prohibitions against, say, drinking not part of the natural order; neither are the concepts underlying laissez-faire capitalism. Justice does not simply happen as a byproduct of a free market; controls and planning by government become increasingly necessary. Furthermore, it is possible that the once-hallowed virtue of productive work ("productive" being narrowly defined in terms of goods and services that are salable on the consumer market) may, amid computerized affluence, become a vice.

This issue of the distinction between genuine natural law and vestigial sectarian morality will become increasingly significant as, in the pluralism of national and world society, men of good will together seek those common structures on which a just, peaceful, and free community of men and nations can be built. In this quest two questions will continue to be raised: How secular (dereligionized or desacralized) can a society become without becoming the victim of a dehumanizing ideology of secularism? And to what extent is a specifically religious ethos —and to what extent should it be—part of the moral consensus which gives coherence to social life?

Two implications become apparent at this point. First, the inclination on the part of the church to think of itself as the only conscience of society must come to an end. A society's conscience will increasingly be the result of dialogue among all ethically-concerned elements within that society. The church must see itself as a contributor to that dialogue, making every effort to upgrade its contribution. Second, with the movement toward a world culture which is pluralistic in character, the church should intensify its dialogue with non-Christian religions and secular ideologies. Attempts at such dialogue between theologians and Marxists in Eastern Europe represent a small but significant beginning. Such a dialogue becomes a common quest for the content of the just and the human which all men are capable of apprehending. The church can ill afford to allow the Christo-logical springs of its motivation in a subtly imperialistic manner to inhibit its affirmation concerning the possibility of such a common quest.

Both Roman Catholic and Protestant thinkers are conceiving a far more dynamic relationship between nature and grace than that set forth in either the Scholastic writings or in the Lutheran or Calvinist confessions. In Roman Catholicism the horizontal line which once separated "nature" on the "ground floor" from "supernature" on the "second story" (a line only penetrated by the sacramental "pipeline") has been blurred almost to the point of obliteration. Such is also the case with the vertical line which in some Lutheran circles separated the redemptive "kingdom on the right hand" (the church) from the nonredemptive "kingdom on the left hand" (the world).

It appears that ethicists are moving toward the place where grace and nature, revelation and reason, love and justice are seen as essentially complementary, as opposite sides of the same coin. The emerging emphasis is less on a sharp separation of love and justice, although the dialectical dimension is by no means lost. Rather, the dialectic has been taken up into an organic understanding which views the two elements as inseparable functions of the divine vitality at work in the world. Thus justice becomes the form which love takes in the world of institutional and corporate relationships. Love serves as that motive power which pushes out the boundaries of justice to include as rights to be guaranteed many of those things which in former generations were considered to fall under the rubric of charity.

Not to be overlooked in this connection is the recent debate over the relationship between *eros* and *agape*. Ever since Nygren's work on the subject, many Lutherans have settled into a habit of mind which considers *eros* as simply a manifestation of sinful, selfish human nature and *agape* as the essence of divine grace in Christ. *Eros* seeks its own, strives for self-justification. *Agape* loves that which is unworthy, is free-flowing, does not strive, but is self-abandoning.

More in keeping with the current trend (and doubtless in part responsible for it) is Paul Tillich's *Love, Power, and Justice*. Tillich asserts that *eros* and *agape*, far from being separate and completely opposite types of love, are in fact two qualities of one reality, love, which along with power and justice have a common ontological ground. Such a view is favored above that of Nygren, especially by thinkers of a psychoanalytic or personalist bent who tend to see different elements in organic interrelation. Such persons hold that the *eros-agape* dichotomy is alien to the biblical witness when taken as a whole. Self-denial (*agape*) has its aspects of self-expression (*eros*); and hatred of self is not an expression of *agape*, but of pride. *Agape* and *eros* are, therefore, dynamic ingredients in the situation of exchange, of giving and receiving again, which characterizes the authentic relationship between persons related to God.

The point being variously made by theologians and ethicists taking this line of approach is that grace—that is, the divine presence and activity which judges and redeems (or recreates) —suffuses all aspects of existence and that wherever new possibilities for human freedom, justice, and fulfillment are found, there are the signs of God's gracious presence and activity on behalf of men. Grace is here understood in terms of both its traditional meanings: God's personal act of forgiving the sinner (the Reformation emphasis) and God's redeeming, enlivening power in the world (the Catholic emphasis). God is the source of power and justice and of love in all its varying qualities. To abstract any of these elements and pit it against another is to do violence to the essential organic unity of Being Itself (Tillich).

This direction of thought has been sufficiently convincing to some theologians that they have gone so far as to suggest that secular institutions and relationships can become—and in some cases are—bearers of redeeming grace. Such potentially grace-bearing social arrangements include racially and economically integrated housing, stepped-up cultural exchange between nations of differing ideologies, and multilateral assistance to developing nations. No such arrangement in itself creates community, but it does afford an opportunity not otherwise available and hence becomes a vehicle for the operation of reconciling grace in secular society. It seems clear that the church, through its educational and missionary enterprises, must make a greater effort at creating the occasions of reconciliation within the church structures and of encouraging them within the secular ones.

As has already been implied, the rapid growth of technology and urbanization has become the occasion for a corresponding growth of optimism within the community of theology and ethics. Lest such optimism become uncritical, a note of caution needs to be sounded. Growth and evolution do not always proceed in a regular or harmonious fashion. Cellular miosis can run away with itself, becoming a cancer that destroys the organism rather than fulfilling it. Social revolution is as likely to devour its own children as it is to establish the justice it set out to achieve. Biological engineering could become a nightmare in the hands of a tyrant, and the destructive potential of thermonuclear energy is all too well known.

This is not simply a matter of an uneven rate in the evolution of social institutions, world community, and a common ethos on the one hand and that of science and technology on the other. Such unevenness, such cultural lag there is to be sure, but the root problem will not be solved simply by closing the gaps. There remains the radical presence of evil, of the daemonic, of sin, of estrangement. This reality, it has been learned too many times in the past, will break out with all the more fury if it is simply covered over by what may be termed an "evolutionary optimism."

In an article celebrating the thought of Teilhard de Chardin, Christopher F. Mooney, S. J., makes the point convincingly. Even as he celebrates the vision of Teilhard de Chardin, Mooney writes that an uncritical acceptance of everything human entails the same type of risk as uncritical rejection. Not everything that develops in the world is an expression of the spirit of Christ. Nor is all human action a search for God. Consequently it is dangerous to state without qualification, as Teilhard does, that the Christian's ultimate goal is that the earth should flourish to the uttermost of its natural powers.

Not long before his death Paul Tillich sounded a similar warning, though in a somewhat different setting. In 1964 at a worldwide conference of thinkers assembled to celebrate and critically to appreciate the encyclical *Pacem in Terris* of Pope John XXIII, Tillich called attention to the daemonic possibilities which, he felt, were all but ignored by the hopeful rationalism on which the encyclical was based. Rationality, he pointed out, is but one ingredient in the creation of world community, just as it is but one ingredient in human politics generally. There are other factors such as power and self-interest which, if they are not in some way accounted for, can readily actualize their irrational daemonic possibilities. Tillich was responding not to an evolutionary but to a neo-Scholastic rationalistic optimism. His point is as pertinent for the first as for the second; any theological view of reality is false and ultimately dangerous if it fails to take account of the daemonic.

A Christian ethics that is both faithful to the church's witness to God's judging and redeeming work and adequate to the present must be attentive to several realities: (1) the dynamic, historical character of God's active presence as set forth in the biblical witness; (2) the essential unity of the divine purpose of redemption along with the diversity of means by which that purpose is accomplished—justice and love, the church and the institutions of the "secular"; (3) the essential freedom-under-God given to the "secular" and its institutions, a freedom that must be protected against all attempts at a bogus religionizing or sacralizing; (4) the pluralistic and in-process character of the world today which requires not a theology of static abstractions but rather a theology of society conceived in terms of organic growth and dynamic interrelationship; and (5) the continued presence of the daemonic with its drive toward fragmentation, heteronomy, and ultimate annihilation.

The whole of evolving reality is today the legitimate datum of theology. The totality of interacting social institutions is the legitimate, indeed, the indispensable datum of Christian ethics. Man is seen as being constituted by his relationships. The increasing complexity of these relationships (with the resulting increasing complexity of the persons constituted by those relationships) leads to the conclusion that Christian ethics today must be social ethics. There can no more be a discontinuity between ethics and society than there can between theology generally and its historical *Sitz im Leben*. It is necessary to develop an ethical methodology which allows for the free course and interrelationships of the myriad forces which give history its movement and through which God, in his law and grace, performs his redemptive work.

As an operation that is essentially hermeneutical, social ethics properly brings its evaluative insights to bear at those points where public social policy is made. Working with understanding gained from the past, as well as with the analytical contribution of the social sciences, social ethics seeks to contribute to the continual reshaping of social policy, not to conform it to an ideological blueprint, but rather, through the genuine taking of risks, to achieve structures which are more open, more human. So we are brought full circle to the assertion mentioned near the beginning of the discussion, which is being made increasingly by Christian ethicists: that to become fully human, to achieve full personhood, man must become "public," "participating" man who is concerned about and committed to those policies and corporate actions that contribute to the increasing realization of human freedom, justice, and community.

Few theologians would question the assertion that God, through the explosive changes now occurring in all areas of life, is speaking a word of eschatological judgment to the church. It is now next to impossible for anyone in the church to hide within the comfortable surroundings of confessional, moralistic, or cultic obscurantism. Going and almost gone are the landmarks of public piety before the tide of pluralism and secularization. Through the radical transformation and, in ever-increasing instances, the utter obliteration of the familiar, God is saying to the church what in other ages he has said through the church. History is open-ended; everything that is, is subject to judgment and to transformation. "Our is not a continuing city."

There is, nevertheless, the continuing danger, noted at various points above, that the old shibboleths will be replaced by new ones and that, in welcoming the challenges of the modern world, the church may unwittingly fix upon that world as the very kingdom of God. The daemonic is ever present and waits for an opportunity to fill all moral vacuums that occur between the rapidly-moving frontiers of science and technology and the more slow-moving frontiers of human sensitivity, insight, and compassion. To welcome scientific and technological advances too naively is to ignore the vacuums and to be caught asleep.

It is therefore to the office of "watchman upon the walls" that the church in every age, and especially in the present one, is called. Her vision requires a clear acquaintance with, by involvement in, secular events and processes. The never-completed task of incisive, prophetic interpretation at the meeting-place of past and future, church and world, individual and society is the unique and vital work of Christian ethics.

# 4

# Ecumenism, History, and Tradition

## I. INTRODUCTION

No other part of the contemporary quest for Christian identity has so galvanized the attention of the world or so aroused the hopes and longing of Christians, both clergy and laity, as the ecumenical movement. Of course, the widespread desire for unity does not consistently spring from strictly theological motivation. Many people have many reasons for wanting ecumenism to flower. Some feel that since confessional allegiance is on the wane and thousands of churchgoers move easily from one denomination to another, the churches are preserving meaningless walls of separation in society. Others feel that in a world where respect is gained primarily through size and power, the institutional church is deeply hindered by its fragmentation. Some are concerned that the anti-Christian forces rampant in our times are too strong for a divided church to withstand. For them union is necessary to promote efficiency and conserve resources.

Many Christians hear a more profound call to ecumenicity in the tensions and the paradoxes of our time. In the light of the overwhelming problems of society, they regard as irresponsible a church that devotes its energies chiefly to institutional maintenance. The population explosion; the growth of fear and distrust among peoples and the consequent destruction of open societies; the accumulation of frightening new arsenals of war; the polarization of power between East and West with the intensification of the possibility of global conflict; the persisting refugee problem; the age-old blights of hunger, ignorance, and disease—all stand over against the yearning for peace, knowledge, freedom, and the full life. Nathan M. Pusey has suggested that the ecumenical movement is perhaps primarily a fresh and vivid renewal of awareness that the church is involved in all of life—that the church has an inescapable responsibility, opportunity, and possibility within itself.

A related and more obviously theological motivation grows out of the desire for the church to be the church. The ecumenical impulse is part of the very nature of Christianity. As God brings humanity to fellowship with himself, he also unites men with one another. Christianity can never exist as the possession of a single individual; it is always a fellowship, that is to say, a church. God has created a fellowship in which a man does not exist for his own sake either in relation to God or to his fellows. Isolation, dissension, and self-sufficiency are exactly contrary to man's true purpose here on earth. K. E. Skydsgaard makes the point that just as there is but one Christ, one cross, one resurrection, so there is only one fellowship, one body, one baptism, and one Eucharist where they can all meet. There is only one Holy Spirit, which creates unity and fellowship. Therefore there cannot be many separated churches of denominations, each with its own confessions, each with its own Lord's Table. From such a viewpoint, ecumenism cannot be a utopian dream. It embraces basic biblical and theological insights that are at the heart of Christianity itself.

"We are partners in that we have heard one and the same comprehensive call," the secretary-general of the World Council of Churches declared to the North American Conference on Faith and Order at Oberlin in 1957. "What you have heard and what I have heard comes from one and the same God who speaks to us in one and the same man, Jesus Christ. We have one and the same hope of our calling—the hope for one and the same kingdom. If God's call to us is one call, that must mean that God sees us as one people, one family. We may draw as many dividing lines as we can, we may organize specific con-

fessions and denominations; in God's sight there is just one body
of those who have heard his call and responded to it; God's
church cannot be divided because its unity belongs to its very
essence."*

The drive toward unity is gradually gaining momentum in
various movements within Christendom. Included are such di-
versities of interest as the liturgical movement, current theological and biblical studies, continuing studies of church history,
and the movement toward the renewal and rededication of the
church to its mission. Running through all of these is the conviction that if the people of God are to be true to their vocation,
they have no choice but to manifest the oneness which is inherent in God himself. Such a unity must be visible to the world
for the sake of the mission of the church.

The dialectic tension between denominational loyalty and ecumenical commitment hinges on the church's concept of itself, a
concept developed chiefly through the church's history and
tradition. In assessing the relationship of tradition to the concept
of Christian unity, it is necessary to look again at the issues
that were at stake at the time of the Reformation. It was here
that western Christendom was splintered and charges were
leveled from both sides that the other had deserted the authentic
tradition and disrupted the continuity of the church. The attempt
is being made in the ecumenical mood of the twentieth century
to heal the division and separation. One of the key issues in the
renewed efforts for the unity of the church is the matter of
identity and continuity. The issues of the sixteenth century were
shaped by historical contingencies and need to be examined
again in the light of 450 years of historical and theological
reflection.

Current theological studies and discussions of both Protestants

*W. A. Viser 't Hooft, "The Ground of Our Unity," *The Nature of
the Unity We Seek: Official Report of the North American Conference on Faith and Order*, ed. Paul S. Minear (St. Louis: Bethany
Press, 1958), pp. 122-24.

and Roman Catholics in the area of Scripture and tradition now make possible a more objective evaluation of the divisive arguments. New viewpoints emerging from the study of the history of dogma help in an examination of the present issues in the context of the long-term development of doctrine and tradition. Ecumenical investigations and studies of the liturgical movement are showing us that Scripture and tradition converge to witness to Christ as the church gathers for the celebration of the gospel. As Roman Catholics are recognizing the indispensable place of preaching in this event, Protestants are recovering a deeper appreciation for the sacraments.

Such examination and study will inevitably point toward specific areas in the developing faith and life of the LCA that deserve attention and action. Several such suggestions are made in the final section of this chapter. Here the concern is expressed that Christian identity and the sense of unity and continuity are in danger of being lost unless the faith, in all its forms and formulations, is reinterpreted and translated into contemporary and relevant concepts and experiences. To do this, the church must accept fully its responsibility to this historical moment, returning to its unchanging source to serve a dramatically changed present.

## II. INTERPRETING THE DEVELOPMENT OF CONFESSIONAL VIEWPOINTS

Tradition has always influenced the formulation of Christian doctrine and the establishment of practices in the Christian community. The earliest Scriptures were preceded by tradition and were based on tradition. Before there was a written record there was the oral transmission. The church remembered Jesus not only in the written record, but also in its sacraments. Dom Gregory Dix reminds us that eucharistic worship at the outset was based not on written Scripture, but solely on tradition.

The first doctrinal decision that the church had to make was which New Testament writings it would accept as normative. By the second century there was quite general agreement on the Gospels and the Epistles of Paul. But the finalization of the canon took several centuries. This decision was based on the traditional usage of the church. The key in that selection was content which testified most accurately to the gospel which the church had received and proclaimed from the beginning. The church lived, preached, baptized, and celebrated the Eucharist for about three centuries before it specified a canon of New Testament writings as an instrument for the exercise of apostolic authority.

Doctrines that were stated obscurely or implicitly in Scripture were, through ensuing centuries, brought to explicit form in the dogmatic pronouncements of the church, so that today we read the Scriptures in this light of traditional interpretation. Tradition and Scripture provide a protection against individualism and guard against private interpretations. Through tradition, the reader of Scripture is both enlightened and guided by the communal wisdom and experience of the church. When one attempts to disregard tradition and return directly to the New Testament, a break in the life of the community occurs, or the community is abandoned and a new one is established. This break is a rejection of the history and the continuing identity of the community. "That which has been believed everywhere, always and by all" cannot be set aside without abandoning the community itself.

The function of tradition is interpretation. But when tradition is dead, it can create a theological rigidity as detrimental as biblical literalism. A living, growing tradition makes possible the appropriation of the ancient formulas and the reinterpretation of these in the context of contemporary concepts and experience. Protestants, more today than ever before, agree with Roman Catholics that extra-scriptural developments are necessary because they are a function of historicity, of the fact that the gospel must be preached and believed in a changing cultural and social milieu. However, Roman Catholics are also recognizing and expressing their general agreement with Protestants that the limits of tradition need to be acknowledged. The self-identity of the church is constituted in history by its tangible and constant memories, hopes, and loyalties. What keeps the church one and the same through all changes is that it always remembers certain specific historical events which culminate in Christ. The church continues to hope for the definite future of the Lord's return.

This historical understanding of the church emphasizes the limits of development and defines clearly that Scripture must be the source and norm for the church's faith and life, because it is the primary witness to the memories and hopes that make the Christian community what it is. This is not to say that the traditions developed over the centuries are to be despised or abandoned. They were the interpretation and the confession of the faith for a particular day in the language and thought forms peculiar to it. They were the translation of the revelation of God to a historical situation.

The sixteenth century debate on Scripture and tradition is not over, but new directions are becoming obvious to both Roman Catholics and Protestants. The debate is now being cast in terms of the relation of Scripture and church. John MacKenzie rightly declares that the identity of gospel and church is not just a book, but that which proclaims Christ. George Lindbeck observes that the Roman Catholic and Protestant emphases in the past can be seen today as more complementary than contradictory. At point after point, it now seems to us, each had hold of part of the truth. But because they operated in a nonhistorical and largely noneschatological framework, they were unable to see that it was only a part. They absolutized their quite correct but partial and inadequate insights.

Historical investigation and theological reflection have compelled many theologians to see the Reformation in the context of the tradition of the church catholic, where the Reformers themselves placed it, and to move backward and forward from the sixteenth century into the entire development of Christian doctrine. One of the interesting results of a re-examination of the writings of the Greek and Latin fathers has been the corroboration of the view of an earlier generation of historical theologians that the focal point of the history of theology, and perhaps of other developments of church history as well, lies in the first five centuries.

Theologians involved in the study of patristics have been confronted with the inescapable necessity for research free from distortion which stems from a particular confessional stance. They have found it not only profitable but also necessary to relate their scholarship to the work of patristic scholars from both Roman Catholic and Eastern Orthodox traditions and to define their task in the ecumenical framework. One of the most significant insights that has grown out of modern scholarship is the recognition of the liturgical setting of the history of doctrine. The interdependence of dogma and ritual in the development of the early church has become evident. The examination of both liturgical and extra-liturgical devotion of these first centuries reveals striking insights into the thought and life of the early church and its self-understanding.

Another important insight is represented by the growing prominence of the history of exegesis and the history of hermeneutics as clues in the assessment of how Christian tradition has developed. In the interpretation of the thought of many figures in the history of theology, a preoccupation with dogmatic or speculative work at the expense of the exegetical has led to serious distortions of their thought. A restoration of the exegetical work to its proper place, therefore, helps to restore balance, proportion, and historical accuracy.

Lutheran theologians and historians traditionally have approached their theological task primarily from the point of the Reformation. But recent patristic study has emphasized a greater sense of continuity in the history of Christian doctrine, with a related intensification of attention to the problem of authority and its development. Jaroslav Pelikan has stated that the problem of continuity in tradition is inescapable, especially for those who believe that the Reformation was a work of God. This brings a new perspective to the question of development of doctrine.

## The History of Dogma

The history of dogma as a theological discipline has the task of interpreting the church's contemporary proclamation in the light of its historical development. This view involves the tacit admission that the doctrinal heritage of the church is subject to historical change, and it is the history of dogma that reflects changes in the self-understanding of the church. The doctrinal development through which Protestantism has passed since the Enlightenment is not the rejection of all earlier doctrinal developments. New forces have set in motion a conflict which often appears chaotic. It has become evident that the tradition which produced Christian doctrine is by no means dead. Fundamental decisions made long ago prove their validity again and again in new situations. The same problems appear over and over again in variety of guises. Valid new solutions can be found only if older solutions are known and evaluated. This points to the need for the history of dogma as a theological discipline. It is part of the essence of Protestantism and a token of its inner vitality that traditional doctrines are subject to continued scrutiny in the light of Scriptures. This examination sometimes produces new theological forms for the age-old content of Christian faith, doctrine, and proclamation.

Agreement on a definition of dogma is not easily reached. The generally accepted definition by Roman Catholics is that dogma is objective truth, revealed by God and defined by the church, either through a conciliar decree, an *ex cathedra* decision of the pope, or by the fact that it is generally taught in the church. In recent years there has been an attempt to define dogma in a broader sense. This newer position is that dogma is simply the prevailing expression of the faith of the Christian community with reference to the content of the Christian revelation. Less importance is attached to precise definitions and ecclesiastical legitimization. In the final analysis such legitimization cannot be regarded as a criterion. What is really important is the Christian self-consciousness.

The difficulty in defining dogma lies chiefly in the fact that the very concept of dogma is historically conditioned and subject to change. Nicaea essentially intended to set forth a confession of faith regarding the consubstantiality of the Son with the Father. Basil the Great first introduced the distinction between kerygma and dogma, but this emphasis did not appear in conciliar action until much later. The dialectic character of dogma first is expressed in the Chalcedon formula of 451. The acknowledgment of dogma in imperial law after Constantine contributed significantly the concept of the infallible character of dogma. It was not until the middle ages that the church developed the doctrine of the *depositum fidei*. This concept maintained that the church had been entrusted with a certain treasury of truth; although none could be lost, the treasure was capable of further development as the ramifications and implications of these truths were made more explicit. The consequence of this doctrine was the church's claim of infallibility for its dogmas at Trent and Vatican I.

Prior to the development of the doctrine of the *depositum fidei* there was an observable continuity in the development of dogma in the early church, beginning with the New Testament. Christ's claims for a confession of himself as Lord and Messiah mark the beginning of this development. And if dogma is interpreted as confession of faith, the continuity in the actions of the church in the succeeding centuries is obvious. It is hardly an accident that the first doctrine to be specified by the Christian church was the doctrine of the Trinity, with an emphasis on the relationship between Son and Father. The development of Christology followed naturally with the definition at Chalcedon of the dogma of the two natures of Christ. It was natural that at approximately the same time the doctrine of sin and grace was clarified in the West, and that during the middle ages the doctrine of the sacraments was further developed. At the time of the Reformation the question concerning the appropriation of salvation became the central problem, one which led to division in western Christianity because it was solved differently by Roman Catholics and Protestants. In our day the question of the unity of the church seems increasingly important, so that perhaps the next steps in the development of the history of doctrine are to be expected in this area.

From the day of Peter's confession to our own there has never been a time when the church has not been called upon to confess its faith. Sometimes this confession was made through the use of the accepted formulas or the ordinary setting of proclamation and sacrament; at other times, as new questions arose and as opposition occurred, new confessions were needed or the old expanded. Thus the historical context of the confession becomes an essential element in its interpretation in a later day. In every instance the matters that called for clarification were essential to the church's witness and its self-understanding. But these actions cannot be interpreted as isolated acts. Only as we acknowledge the continuity in their development can we translate the past and create, in the present, confessions that speak to contemporary questions and tasks.

The continuity of confessional development also raises the question of the authority of dogmas or confessions. The Reformation writings gave dogmas or confessions two functions. They were to summarize or set forth the teaching of Scripture, and thus were always subject to Scripture and always tested and interpreted in the light of Scripture. They also were to provide guidance for the interpretation of Scripture by directing the interpreter away from error and emphasizing the central biblical message. The authority of dogmas or confessions, in this sense, is not to be stated in terms of their infallibility, but rather in terms of their compelling nature. Their authority rests in their ability to actualize the confession of Christ in the face of problems of a given day.

Any discussion of the authority of confessional statements cannot ignore the fact that the church has always been under the conviction that it is led by the Holy Spirit. There is no way in which the church can prove the help of the Spirit, nor can it deny that it has erred in the past. But an insight which the church has gained, in human weakness and in historically contingent form to be sure, but yet with the help of the Holy Spirit, must be taken seriously. Nor is it right to make temporary relevance the measure of dogma. Certain confessions of the past may suddenly regain an entirely unexpected relevance. In the struggle of the German church with National Socialism not only the Barmen Declaration but also the dogmas and confessions of the ancient church and of the Reformation spoke to the church. The continuity of the history of dogma has its basis in the continuity of the church, to which God has promised the Holy Spirit for every age.

Although the Roman Catholic church claims infallibility for its dogmas, there are a growing number of Catholic theologians who insist that this infallibility does not imply an absolute finality and perfection of defined dogmas. They maintain that the church's failure to recognize the historical contingencies under which doctrine was formulated has produced an atmosphere in which the question of the reinterpretation of dogma spreads unrest in Catholic circles. This is the result of the custom of viewing the understanding of truth in a purely conceptualistic way. The real problem in the Roman Catholic reinterpretation of dogma is that its doctrine of infallibility insists that, although the dogma may be expanded, its objective content cannot be changed. However, some theologians feel that doctrines can be assimilated into a new self-understanding, and thereby be given a new and different function in the whole of the totality of faith.

What implications this concept will have for handling such problems as those created by the dogmas of infallibility and Mariology the whole Protestant world waits eagerly to see.

Yet it is not exclusively the problem of Roman Catholic theologians. It is also ours. The serious pursuit of the history of dogma, spurred by historical and existential thinking, may yet enable Roman Catholics and Protestants to confess their faith in new forms that do not discard the old, but recognize their validity for that time and situation. An important role for the history of dogma in the future theological task will be to demonstrate the evidences of continuity and discontinuity in the development of doctrine. As Protestants and Catholics recognize how they have shared in both, perhaps new doors will be opened.

## The Present Situation

If theology is to be intelligible, it has to use the language of the culture within which it is formed. It cannot escape the influence of the mentality, intellectual climate, or the religious concerns of its culture. Secular influences cannot be avoided, and secular concerns are essential if its address is to be relevant. This means that there can be no finally fixed theology. It must be reformulated by each generation. Theology is always culturally conditioned, and as cultural forms change it must engage in reinterpretation. The cosmology, psychology, and the social conditions of one era become unintelligible to another. While the primary revelation in the Christian faith remains the same, with Scripture and tradition both serving to prevent irresponsible innovations, there is element in theology that must address itself to its own day in the language and terms of its cultural forms.

Christian identity reflects the character of both change and permanence—both *history* and *tradition*. The fact that the Christian faith is a historical religion implies a dynamic quality. The contingencies of history shape its form and its language, although it has its basis in a revelation that is constantly re-presented in

Scripture and tradition. As it returns to that initial revelatory experience, it is confronted with an event that has permanent and universal validity.

In our day it seems to many that the desire to be relevant for the sake of relevance and modernity has led some theologians to accommodate the revelation to the current mood and to merge its content into our cultural forms. Karl Barth pointed to the danger when he observed that man is tempted to take the divine into his possession and to bring it under his management. However, Paul Tillich defended his procedure of stating theology in forms derived from the prevailing culture. He specified his awareness of the danger that in this way the substance of the Christian message may be lost. He felt that the danger must be risked, for dangers are not a reason for avoiding a serious demand.

John MacQuarrie argues for maintaining a balance between the given and permanent revelation and the historical contingency of changing culture. He points out that if the demand for relevance and intelligibility is to be met, then there will always be a danger of infringing the autonomous character of revelation. This must be weighed against the other danger of insulating the revelation against all contact with the changing forms of secular culture. Lutheranism, in its official and formal theological positions, has frequently avoided, if not opposed, the demand to be relevant to contemporary culture. Often its theology has been marked by a static confessionalism and its piety by inherited cultural forms of another era. Officially it has held firmly to its confessions and its Reformation inheritance, but its reluctance or inability to reinterpret these in terms of its new historical involvements and responsibilities has often vitiated their influence and effect, not only upon formal theology but also upon the life of the churches and the people. Jaroslav Pelikan has voiced concern that American Lutheranism may thereby lose its catholic substance and its identity as a confessional church and move toward becoming just another denomination.

As immigrant churches, American Lutherans evidenced no

common attitude toward their confessional history. Extremes of preoccupation and unconcern were both present. In many ways the American Lutherans have been influenced and shaped by their contacts with other Protestant groups as much as by Roman Catholic tradition and their heritage of the Reformation. Although this influence has often separated them from their ecumenical and confessional roots, it has been more an unconscious transformation than a conscious one.

Symptoms of this loss of identity as a confessional church can be cited in several areas of its life and faith. Although the ecumenical creeds are used in Lutheran worship, Lutheran preaching and piety too often reflect a "unitarianism of the second person" that obscures the catholic and Reformation understanding of the Triune God. A preoccupation with the second article makes church vulnerable to a reductionist theology that eliminates everything except the figure of Jesus. Even when the doctrine of justification does receive proper treatment, a lack of emphasis on the doctrine of creation distorts the proclamation of the gospel. A world that has experienced a revolution in the social and physical sciences cannot develop a theology adequate for its day apart from the biblical concept of God and the biblical concept of a universal history in which the Christ-event is properly understood as the key.

Too little attention is given to the Old Testament in Lutheran preaching and teaching. Current biblical studies demonstrate that the Old Testament is indispensable for the proper interpretation and understanding of the New Testament. The universality of God's plan for mankind is pictured in the Old Testament as nowhere else. Pannenberg states the case strongly when he observes that only the almighty and yet faithful God of Israelitic tradition gave rise to an understanding of reality as a history of ever-new events. It may be doubted whether history can be understood as a unity without knowledge of the one biblical God. John Cobb makes a similar claim for the historical dimensions of the Old Testament in stating his belief that it will become increasingly clear that the history of Israel is central to human history and that it is culminated and transformed in Jesus Christ. If the redemptive work of God in Christ is to become a relevant message to modern man, it must be set in the context of universal history as witnessed in the *whole* biblical tradition.

The provision in the Lutheran liturgy for the reading of an Old Testament selection was an important step in the right direction, but no significant use of these texts for preaching is evident. However, with or without suitable lectionary readings, the great texts and themes of the Old Testament deserve to be expounded from Lutheran pulpits. Its eschatological dimensions, its declaration for God's universal rule and concern, and its passion for social justice can address modern man in terms that demonstrate the meaning of his own existence in history.

## Liturgical Renewal

Sacramental and liturgical studies have become a significant area of investigation and re-evaluation for both Catholics and Protestants. The search for Christian identity ultimately leads all seekers to that place and that experience where God's word can be heard and where his presence can be known. The worship of the gathered community is the life-situation in which the Spirit brings to remembrance today all that God has done for his people and mankind yesterday. Through word and sacrament, hymn and prayer, the church, the body of Christ, experiences his living presence through the Spirit. The liturgy becomes a means for transmitting the tradition of witness to Jesus Christ. It is an essential link between the past and the present.

Concern with liturgy is not a peripheral matter. The history of religion reminds us that every society effects its unity and transmits its communal life more effectively through common rituals which celebrate its objects of devotion than through formal organization or instruction. Christianity lives in and through the memory of the acts and promises of God, of the Exodus out of

Egypt and the new exodus into the new age which occurred in Christ's death and resurrection. It is in worship, the liturgical celebration of these memorials and hopes which involves the active participation of the whole congregation, that the community exists most intensely and existentially. As Christians enact their remembrance of what Christ has done and will do, the Lord is most fully and substantially present.

In worship the experience of the past is actualized and the future pre-actualized in the sacrament of Christ's presence. The eschatological implication of the sacrament enables the Christian to recognize the meaning of his existence in terms of a universal history. Past, present, and future are bridged in that communion. Because Catholics and Protestants are thinking in terms which are both more biblical and more modern than in the past, there is an encouraging common effort in the area of sacramental and liturgical theology.

The critical reverence of Lutheranism toward the Catholic substance of its past seems so apparent in the matter of liturgy and worship as to need little comment. Lutherans may regard ceremonies as matters of indifference theologically, but they do not regard such ceremonies with indifference. Luther refused to let his fundamental insight into the priority of the means of grace blind him to the significance and value of symbolic actions in the life and worship of the church. Moreover, in his estimation liturgy provided a sense of identity and continuity with the life of the whole communion of saints. It helped a man to relate himself to both the world of culture and the world of nature. Pelikan concludes that Luther's liturgical views and productions are evidence of his continuing awareness of Catholic substance.

The so-called liturgical movement or liturgical renewal (so-called because it is consciously not an organization or a program) is yet another attempt to give expression to Christian identity. Although its expression sometimes degenerates into an antiquarian concern with what is "proper" in the public worship of God, it is basically an effort to express in the life of the people of God the nexus between secular life and the on-going history of the people of God. In contrast to those who speak of the "non-church," liturgical renewal sees the worship of the congregation as central, whether the entire congregation is assembled in one place or smaller units of the congregation are meeting in homes or places of work. This liturgical pattern has essentially two aspects—the church in assembly and the church in dispersion. This "going out" and this "coming in" provide a basic rhythm of liturgical life which is repeated every time the liturgy is celebrated. Christians come together to receive the Lord and go out to celebrate his presence in the world. The liturgical movement has shown that this rhythm ought to be expanded into a pattern of liturgical life which takes place partly in the large assemblies when the whole church is drawn together and partly in small groups in dispersion.

As the liturgical movement has developed, it has become increasingly theological and ethical in its concerns. Its concern is for the whole life and mission of the church and the meaningful expression of that life and mission in the "liturgy" of the people of God. It maintains that the Christian life cannot be compartmentalized. Whatever a Christian does, the celebration of the liturgy or the living service of his fellowmen, is properly labeled as worship. This is not to say that man is given a choice between two roads down which he may travel as he responds to God's grace. *Leiturgia* (or cultus) and *diakonia* (or ethics) are not mutually exclusive. It is not a case of either/or but of both/and. There has been a shift from tradition for its own sake —the externals of ceremonialism, religious individualism, and the exclusively Roman Catholic tradition—to a much more factual knowledge of the basis of liturgy, an awareness of the role of the laity, a concern for society, a concern for church unity, an awakening to the mission of the church, a realization of the church as the body of Christ, and a renewed awareness of the Bible.

Study and experimentation are going on in a variety of directions: recovery and interpretation in contemporary form of the original meaning of the traditional Christian liturgy; experimentation with new forms of the liturgy for the gathered congregation, with special emphasis on the sacraments; experimentation with "para-liturgies" designed to communicate the gospel in dramatic form to those outside the church; experimentation with forms of cultus for new expressions of the Christian community, such as the "house church" and the community gathered around places of work. In all of this experimentation there are three major emphases:

—reintegration and wholeness, the unification of all of the life of the Christian, both in the church and in the world;

—participation of all of the people in the life of the Christian community, as opposed to the liturgical passivity which has become characteristic of both Roman Catholic and Protestant churches;

—the doctrine of the priesthood of Christ as the key both to the reintegration and wholeness of life.

The liturgical movement is essentially ecumenical. While various denominations have departments responsible for worship and liturgical groups within the denominational fellowship, there is a great deal of communication across denominational lines as well as across Roman Catholic-Protestant lines. There is an increasing unity of agreement in this communication. The common concern is to discover a Christian "style of life" which is truly expressive of the gospel life at mid-twentieth century.

Even though the liturgical movement has shown significant strength and influence in some areas of the church, much education needs to take place. Greater emphasis must be placed on the proper relation of the Word and sacrament. In addition to the need for preaching to be more biblical there is equally a need for worship to be truly eucharistic. For twenty centuries the sacrament has been a bulwark against intellectualism and individualism in the church. The dramatic action of the sacrament is a needed complement to the oral proclamation.

It is interesting to note that the LCA Commission on Worship reported at a recent meeting that congregations that are becoming most concerned about the proper relationship of Word and sacrament as the basis and content of their worship are also becoming the most active in social concerns. Those who have been in Christ's presence seem to be most committed to being Christ's presence in the world about them. Perhaps this is the day for Lutherans to return to the tradition of the fathers; if not in form, at least in substance.

The Lutheran service has retained the Holy Communion as an integral part of the weekly worship—in the book, but not in reality. It elected to officially entitle the communion The Thanksgiving, but in the minds of most Lutherans the observance is more penitential than eucharistic. Only a small number of LCA parishes provide for a weekly communion. One Lutheran seminary professor aptly described the situation when he stated that "some Lutheran churches still bar from their communion those who do not hold the same interpretation of the doctrine of the Real Presence, but they usually cannot bar them more than once a month."

### III. ORGANIZATIONAL MANIFESTATIONS OF ECUMENICAL CONSCIOUSNESS

There is general recognition today that unity is the gift of God and the work of the Holy Spirit, not the achievement of man. Hidden in such a confession is the admission that unity is a spiritual event involving renewal and a change of heart, not simply cooperation without change. The churches have discovered that they possess in common the general creeds, the Scriptures, forms of worship, baptism, and a discipline of life rooted in love. They have learned that unity is fostered not by overlooking differences but through facing them honestly and without apology. On the other hand they have discovered that, procedurally, unity can best be reached not by focusing on the differences but through re-examination together of the basic nature of the church and its teachings, particuarly as these are proclaimed in the Scriptures.

Already the ecumenical movement has revealed areas where cooperation and a common front can be achieved. As early as 1922, Life and Work addressed Faith and Order with the plea: "In the region of moral and social questions we desire all Christians to begin at once to act as if they were one body in one visible fellowship. This can be done by all alike without injury to theological principles. We are concerned with service, and we believe that by serving the cooperation of churches we shall break down prejudices and create a spirit of fellowship which will render the accomplishment of the aims of the Faith and Order Movement less difficult to achieve." Although there has been considerable caution in relation to this "as-if" theory, its spirit has been incorporated into almost all ecumenical organizations and has provided the ground for a growing number of cooperative social service projects.

Perhaps more important, the ecumenical movement has led to changes within the thinking, structures, and programs of individual churches that enable them to walk toward each other. Father Gregory Baum has cited three changes in the Roman Catholic church arising from ecumenical influences: the architectural design of church buildings, sacramental theology, and the character of devotional literature prepared for the use of the laity. Each change has tended to make closer relationships possible between Roman Catholics and Protestants. Another evidence of the growing readiness to accept that which is worthy in other traditions is the list of principles in Catholic and Reformed tradition cited by Eugene Carson Blake and subsequently considered in the Consultation on Church Union. These principles include:

—visible and historic continuity with the church of all ages;
—confession of the historic trinitarian faith received from the apostles and set forth in the Apostles' and Nicene Creeds;

—the administration of the two dominical sacraments of Baptism and the Lord's Supper;

—acceptance of the principle of continuing reformation under the word of God by the guidance of the Holy Spirit;

—the maintenance of a church truly democratic in its government;

—and a willingness to include within its catholicity (and because of it) a wide diversity of theological formulations of the faith and variety in worship.

The Consultation on Church Union that has resulted from the Blake Proposal is one more indication of the unity the churches already possess in Christ. "We could not seek union if we did not already possess unity," William Temple said at Edinburgh in 1937. "Those who have nothing in common do not deplore their estrangement."

Other expressions of the unity the churches already possess may be gathered under five headings:

A. *Expressions within confessional and denominational boundaries.* Examples are the mergers that created the Lutheran Church in America, The American Lutheran Church, and the United Presbyterian Church in the United States. On a global scale are the developments of the Lutheran World Federation, the World Presbyterian Alliance, the World Methodist Conference, the Baptist World Alliance, and the Lambeth Conference, which bring together national church bodies sharing common allegiances.

B. *Expressions among denominations.* Chief exhibits here are the United Church of Canada, the Church of Christ in Japan, and the Church of South India. Eighteen such mergers have been consummated since 1910. The most impressive effort in the United States is still in progress in the Consultation on Church Union. Ten denominations presently are represented. Several other denominations have sent observers to sessions of the consultation. Present plans call for ratification of basic principles and union by 1980, to be followed by thirty years of federation. Development of a constitution is projected during the federation period.

C. *Expressions on a national basis through a federation of denominations.* The prime example is the National Council of Churches of Christ in the U.S.A., organized in 1950 as an agency through which Christian churches might do together that which could not be done as well, if at all, separately. It is composed of Protestant, Anglican, Old Catholic, and Eastern Orthodox communions. Represented are most major Christian bodies in the United States except the Roman Catholic. The conciliar movement provides opportunity at every level for inter-church discussion and action. Local and national councils of churches, as well as the World Council, have been organized. In addition to such council machinery, a growing array of interdenominational conferences have been arranged to deal with theological inquiry on a joint basis. Examples are in the series of meetings between Lutheran and Catholic theologians in Germany, Lutheran and Reformed theologians in America and Europe, and the International Theological Conference held at Notre Dame University, March 1966, to provide an interfaith appraisal of Vatican II.

D. *Expressions on a global scale among churches.* In 1947 the World Council of Churches brought together the Faith and Order Movement, which met for the first time at Lausanne in 1927, and the Life and Work Movement, which held its first meeting in 1925 in Stockholm. Then at New Delhi in 1961, the World Council merged with the International Missionary Council, which had organized in 1921. Each body and movement brought to the council a particular concern. Faith and Order sought the basis for furthering unity through the examination of doctrinal differences and agreements among the church. Life and Work grew out of the concern for the church's role and responsibility in social needs and world affairs. The International Missionary Council sought to coordinate Protestant world mission activities and to supply ecumenical leadership.

The World Council of Churches is as representative a body of churches as the world has yet seen. In the words of its provisional committee, it seeks "to promote this unity (the longing for one church among all Christians) among its members and to serve them as an organ whereby they may bear witness together to their common faith and cooperate in matters requiring united action." A number of departments implement the joint concerns of the member churches in such areas as theological study, inter-church aid, social needs, international affairs, and the exploration of new opportunities for joint action. John A. Mackay has observed that the World Council of Churches has become the symbol and dynamic center of efforts directed towards the visible expression of Christian unity. Although the continued movement of the churches toward complete unity through this organization brings the dangers inherent in a mammoth organization, there is no question that the role of the council in ecumenical affairs has increased impressively since its formation.

E. *The new rapprochement between Protestantism and the Roman Catholic church.* Although conversations between Roman Catholic and Protestant churchmen have been going on for many years on the continent, particularly between Lutherans and Roman Catholics in Germany, the new openness and ecumenical consciousness on the part of Roman Catholicism is an outgrowth of Vatican II. Samuel McCrea Cavert views the Decree on Ecumenism as the beginning of a new age in the relation of the churches to one another—an age that can truly be called ecumenical. The ecumenical movement which developed outside of Roman Catholicism for fifty years prior to the summoning of Vatican Council II by Pope John XXIII was truncated by the lack of Catholic participation. The Council awakened hopes that there might be a change in Catholic attitude. Those hopes have now been fulfilled beyond all expectations.

Such optimism seems warranted by a number of characteristics and elements in the decree. One of these is the new manner in which it speaks of non-Catholic Christians. Granting them respect and paying fair attention to their position, it recognizes that "truly Christian endowments" may be found outside the Roman Catholic church. Another is stress on "the task of renewal and reform" as essential to ecumenical advance. Still another is the recognition that "men on both sides were to blame" for the present schisms in the church. An additional sign of hope is the strong emphasis on the Scripture and the implied assumption of its centrality in tradition.

The decree announces that "in certain special circumstances" it is "allowable, indeed desirable," that Catholics "join in prayer with their separated brethren." It commends "cooperation among all Christians" and suggests that it be "increasingly developed" in relation to the problems of contemporary society. Perhaps the most encouraging characteristic of the entire decree is its commitment to dialogue in the future. Although we still stand too close to Vatican II to plot with any degree of accuracy the future pathway of Roman Catholic relationships with other Christian churches, no account of the present state of ecumenism can overlook the fact that Catholic openness is the great new fact in ecumenical developments.

Before the unity of the church is achieved, the ecumenical movement must progress much farther than it has. Much has been accomplished in the past. But many and large problems lie ahead. Only a few of these problems are stated and examined briefly below.

The recognition the churches have given to one another is often tentative and incomplete. The Toronto statement of the World Council acknowledges that member churches "do not necessarily recognize each other as true, healthy, or complete churches." Instead, "they consider the relation of other churches to the *Una Sancta* as a question for mutual consideration." The Orthodox churches and those recognizing the historic episcopacy as an indispensable mark of the church find even their membership in councils of churches a difficulty in the light of their ecclesiological doctrine.

The ecumenical movement lacks a theology with which to guide choices and against which to evaluate actions. Visser 't Hooft has isolated this theological problem by asking the following questions: What is the relationship of the churches in this movement? Is it an expression of a real unity? If so, how is it related to the unity of which the New Testament speaks? How can that unity which the churches already possess grow toward a more complete unity?

Other theological problems provide continuing points of difference in the ecumenical dialogue. Protestants still disagree over baptism. And it still is difficult to arrange a communion service in which all Protestant representatives at an ecumenical gathering will participate. Another major problem for Protestants is the historic episcopacy. Early in this century, Lutheran Archbishop Nathan Söderblom, guiding spirit of the Life and Work Movement, insisted that the real frontier in the union problem was the episcopal doctrine of the church, between those who consider the historic episcopal office necessary to the true congregation of Christ, and those who do not. In the wide reaches of Catholic-Protestant relationships lie the unresolved problems of the papacy and the role of Mary in church dogma.

Another problem is caused by the fact that some church leaders have become so compulsive about unity that they have become blinded to the necessity of dealing with other problems confronting the church. In addressing the New Delhi meeting of the World Council of Churches on the quest for unity, Anglican Archbishop A. M. Ramsey used John 17 as the basis of his remarks. Pointing out Christ's concern there for truth, unity, and holiness, he said that the world does not hear the call to holiness and does not care for the truth in Christ. The world has its own desire for unity conceived in a secular way. It desires that men and nations be joined together and the forces which separate them removed. The world, caring for unity, is shocked when the church fails to manifest it. While the world's criticism must rightly humble us, we must not necessarily accept the world's conception of unity. It is not just unity, togetherness with one another, that we seek; although ecclesiastics have sometimes slipped into talking as if it were and have isolated unity from the other notes of the church. It is for unity in truth and holiness that we work and pray—that is, Christ's supernatural gift to us. A movement which concentrates on unity as an isolated concept can mislead the world and mislead us, as indeed would a movement which was concerned exclusively with holiness or truth.

Precisely at the point of theological difference another dissension arises. Some within the ecumenical movement say that organizational union should precede theological unity. They claim that what unites all Christians now is adequate for visible unity. On the other side of the fence are those who insist that union in the face of doctrinal differences involves a loss of integrity. They say it is a violation of conscience that can ultimately lead only to betrayal of the faith.

Considerable confusion is caused by the fact that not everyone concerned with the need for Christian unity has the same set of goals in mind. For some, unity does not necessarily involve organizational relatedness. To them unity is invisible in its ideal nature. No visible structure to manifest such unity is needed or even desirable. For others, unity consists ideally of a federation of the churches. In such an organization each body could maintain its own flavor and identity, yet cooperate in many areas of church life. For still others, unity has an organic quality essential to the very construct of the church. To them the only faithful consummation of the ecumenical movement would be a structurally united, visible church organization.

The World Council itself, as the chief symbol of ecumenical activity, presents problems. To many people ecumenism means belonging to the World Council of Churches or some other interchurch organization. This is not the full meaning of ecumenism. As originally conceived, the ecumenical movement held a vision of one church of Jesus Christ visibly gathered together to fulfill its one calling and had little to do with organizations of any kind.

Warning that the World Council of Churches has succeeded almost too well as an institution, Bridston notes two dangers that face it. First is the danger of conservatism that always marks institutions. Second is the danger, despite its effort not to become a "superchurch," of turning into a "superorganization" with some of the worst traits of ecclesiastical life. He lists a series of challenges that face the council from within its own structure: how to move beyond structures and procedures "too woodenly agendized"; how to prevent unity from becoming captured and domesticated by the churches; how to maintain openness and flexibility toward new ideas and new developments; how to avoid introverted, esoteric cliquism; and how to become institutionalized without ceasing to be a movement.

From outside its structure the World Council faces the challenge of natural and regional isolation, unilateral confessionalism and denominational consolidation, ethical and cultural self-sufficiency, and the existence of large groups of Christians outside its dialogue.

Denominationalism's whole magnetic field of emotions cannot be easily rearranged by a countercurrent of logic. Denominational loyalties that have become a part of both the institutional and religious life of many people cannot be wiped out by fiat. People have built their lives around sincere convictions with respect to faith and practice within their denominations. To submit these convictions to review is to question the foundations of their lives. Such re-examination threatens the value of years of spiritual and moral discipline.

Finally, the ecumenical movement must define and maintain its boundaries. Presently it limits itself to activities among Christian churches. But some sincerely believe that the lines must be extended. When Rabbi Arthur Gilbert joined the editorial staff of the *Journal of Ecumenical Studies*, Lutheran George Lindbeck applauded the move and justified his position by pointing to the eschatological and prophetic elements of Jewish faith and life. "For us . . . the first great schism was the one which occurred in the New Testament times between Jew and Christian," he said. "It is inconsistent for us to seek to heal later divisions without wrestling also with the original rupture. There is, in Christian circles, a growing conviction that many of our ills stem from forgetfulness of our Jewishness. This is manifest, not only in the appalling ills of Christian anti-Semitism, but also in the neglect of the eschatological and prophetic dimensions of our faith."*

Max Thurian, brother in the Taizé community, raises the question of relations between Christianity and all world religions. He makes the point that the church cannot automatically reject all people or groups outside its own visible unity. It must rejoice in truth and unity wherever these are found and recognize these as also of God. The church knows that Christ died for *all* men, and that he wishes them all in the unity of his body. But the church cannot tell in advance how this redemption and this unity are to be applied. It is asked only to be itself—the body of Christ, the presence in the world of the humanity of our Lord. It must extend the presence of this humanity of Christ everywhere, offering itself to God as an obedient instrument for his work.

Ecumenism may choose to pursue one of several concepts of unity. Samuel McCrea Cavert lists the possibilities as the unity of spiritual fellowship, the unity of cooperative association and action, the unity of mutual recognition, and the unity of a single church. Many feel that only the last concept, looking toward one church with a common doctrinal basis and a common administrative structure, fulfills the conditions for the one church described in the New Testament. Others fear, however, that such organization would bring centralization, uniformity, and a rigid authoritarianism inconsistent with the spirit of the New Testament.

Cavert claims that this fear need not be actualized. Organic

---

*George Lindbeck, "Jewish-Christian Dialogue I," *Journal of Ecumenical Studies*, III (Winter 1966), p. 146.

union does not necessitate centralized control, he maintains. A body is an organism that consists of mutually connected and mutually dependent parts, constituted to function as a living whole. Organic unity exists when a single stream of life flows through all the parts and when no part is shut off from any aspect of the common experience. Organic unity of the churches does require interchangeable membership, so that a Christian who belongs to any congregation can be received as a member of any other congregation, a ministry which is everywhere accepted as the ministry of the entire church, and sacraments of universal validity to which all church members are welcome. The great difficulty in achieving unity which would include these three things is immediately apparent. For most churches membership, ministry, and the sacraments are all at the core of denominational identity.

That the future is not all bleak is evident in the growing emphasis in all communions on a common approach to the church as the people of God and the body of Christ—concepts that have grown in stature as a result of recent biblical studies. Strong emphasis, for example, was given to these ideas in the decree on the church adopted by Vatican II. Some progress has also been made in sacramental theology, particularly in its sacrificial aspects. The sacrifice of the mass in Catholicism is seen by some to be a part of the whole deed of God in Christ offered once for all but with continuing effect. The key to solving the problem of a common ministry may lie in the new stress on the ministry of the laity, which also received considerable attention at Vatican II. This subject is being studied afresh both jointly and individually by nearly all denominations with ecumenical concerns.

No corporate union with common doctrine and a single administrative structure seems desirable on either a global or a national scale. On the one hand, the world is too large and complex for a single church government. On the other hand, the development of an American church as over against a German church as over against a Japanese church as over against an

English church carries so many overtones of nationalism that it probably should be avoided. Much more preferable would be a visible form of unity characterized by the three conditions proposed by Cavert.

## IV. LUTHERANISM AND ECUMENISM

Where do the Lutheran churches stand with respect to the ecumenical movement? What are prospects for their participation in ecumenical activities in the immediate future?

The strong role that Lutherans have played in the movement is evident by merely scanning the list of ecumenical leaders. Nathan Söderblom was the father of the Life and Work movement. Franklin Clark Fry was chairman of the Central Committee of the World Council of Churches from 1954 to 1968. O. Frederick Nolde has been director of the World Council's efforts in international affairs since the council's formation. Rajah B. Manikam was the first East Asia secretary of the joint World Council-International Missionary Council office.

Lutherans probably will continue to insist that agreement in essentials of faith and doctrine must precede any kind of organic union. On the other hand, Lutherans have become willing to sit with representatives of other denominations to re-examine together the foundations of faith in the search for new formulations of its truths. As almost everywhere in Christendom—among Lutherans too—the walls of isolation have cracked. A fresh willingness to listen to the insights and appreciate the contributions of other traditions marks the leadership of the church. Apparent is a readiness to examine how much of the wall of separation consists of differences over essentials of faith and doctrine and how much it consists of cultural, economic, national, and emotional factors. But even more attention needs to be paid to recognizing the various factors of separation for what they are and to evaluating their relevance to the faith.

It seems obvious that the hope for the resolution of disagreements continues to lie in a return to the sources of faith and doctrine. To foster this return the Lutheran Church in America might increase the denominational scope of such theological discussions as those that have recently been conducted with Presbyterians, and a wider range of historical, liturgical, and theological aspects of church life might be considered in the discussion. In addition, the Board of Theological Education and the Board of World Missions might be encouraged to foster, both in America and overseas, ventures in cooperative theological education parallel to those in Rajahmundry, Chicago, and Singapore, and the synods might be nudged toward a more favorable attitude toward the graduates of institutions engaging in such ventures in cooperative education.

The Commission on Evangelism, the Board of American Missions, the Board of Social Ministry, the Board of World Missions, and other units of the church may find promise in experimentation which involves the laity in new forms of ecumenical Christian service and ministry.

Insight into the mission of the church need not always keep us apart. It could bring us together. To the extent that Christian congregations of whatever denomination are fulfilling the mission of God, they may attempt to do so together. Defensiveness concerning denominational identity on a local level may be exposed as being unnecessary, as congregations experiment with cooperation in fulfilling various aspects of the mission of the church.

Lutheran-Roman Catholic relationships deserve special attention because of the particular historical relationship between the two communions. The conservative nature of the Lutheran Reformation provides a helpful perspective. Wilhelm Pauck points out that it was undertaken with the intention of preserving all customs, traditions, rites, and doctrines that were not clearly in conflict with the Word. Thus Lutheran church order continued the stream of Roman Catholic historical tradition precisely because it was a corrective reformation of Roman Catholicism.

The attempt was made to renew the church in the context of Roman Catholic ecclesiastical and religious life by purging it of its unevangelical accretions and corruptions.

Jaroslav Pelikan develops the point that the true church of Christ needs both "Catholic substance" and "Protestant principle." Catholic substance is regarded as the body of tradition, liturgy, dogma, and churchmanship of the Roman Catholic church of Luther's day insofar as it squared with the gospel. Protestant principle is the criticism and reconstruction of Catholic substance carried out by Luther on the basis of the gospel and the authority of the Bible. The key to a contemporary renewal of the church is a dual emphasis on both Catholic substance (historical tradition) and Protestant principle (informed historical criticism).

Pelikan maintains that Catholic substance and Protestant principle are both embedded in Luther's view of the church. He saw the church as both the body of Christ in a theological sense and as an empirical and historical institution, with the imperfections which are inevitable in such institutions. The one church was both visible and invisible. Luther rejected both the Roman Catholic identification of the empirical church with true communion of saints and the radical Protestant view that individual authority replaces the authority of the church in matters religious. In Lutheran theology, history—including the church and the church's witness—is viewed as the conditioned bearer of the activity of God. Lutheranism is not afraid of historical criticism, because it does not posit infallibility for the historical church. When historical study uncovers theological misunderstandings or corruption in the church at a given time or place, the validity of the church is not destroyed.

Pelikan sees the twofold emphasis on Catholic substance and Protestant principle reflected in the Augsburg Confession's twofold view of tradition. The confession used the plural of *traditio* to translate *Menschensatzungen*, "human traditions, instituted to placate God, to merit grace, to make satisfaction for sins." The negative connotation is used to emphasize the Protestant principle of biblical authority. However, the traditionalism of the confession is conspicuous when it deals with the received Catholic substance of the past. There are abundant and explicit protestations of loyalty. This includes adherence to the ancient creeds.

Luther's evangelical catholicity manifested itself in a distinctive interpretation of church councils. Luther cried out in appeal for a council of the church, beseeching all Christendom for its advice and help. His basic thesis was that decrees of genuine councils must remain in force permanently, especially regarding the primary concern with which each council dealt. Accidental, temporal, external, and temporary matters to which councils addressed themselves were not to be regarded on a par with crucial matters of faith and doctrine. For example, faithfulness to Nicaea meant affirmation of its conclusions about its primary concern—the doctrine that Christ is true God. It did not require acceptance and enforcement of regulations about a contemporary temporal problem—the defection of soldiers. Luther maintained that the decisions of the apostolic council and of the ecumenical councils on the primary concern facing each of them were permanently binding. Other decisions were binding only as long as the conditions which called them forth still obtained.

Luther's reservations about the final authority of councils of the church stemmed from his lack of confidence in the leadership and organization of particular councils rather than from a rejection of the institution itself. He insisted that councils could err, and that they did err when their decisions were contrary to Scripture. The final authority for the church and for Christians must be the Scriptures, not a council.

A review of Lutheran history suggests that Lutheran churches are following a pattern of seeking to achieve organic unity among themselves on a national level and federated unity among themselves on an international level. In the past the achievement of such unity has been regarded as prerequisite to unity and merger with other evangelical communions. The time may have come, however, to evaluate the extent to which Lutheran denomi-nationalism is masquerading as Lutheran confessionalism to the detriment of Christian confessionalism.

We should make central to our ecumenical activity the search to discover and the effort to fulfill the mission of the church of Christ. This compulsion should drive us and inhibit us. It should drive us to work constantly to bring about the unity for which Christ prayed. It should inhibit us from thinking we have found that unity in anything less than the living out of the mission of God. Our task, therefore, is to search for and to accept and to cooperate with and to claim the fellowship of the church wher-ever we find it, whatever label it wears.

Jaroslav Pelikan has observed that Lutherans have begun to learn that the only base broad enough to support confessional loyalty and to rescue it from sectarian debasement is an ecu-menical Christendom. A church that seeks to save its life shall lose it, but a church that is willing to give itself to the total life of the whole church will receive its own life back. The Lutheran tradition is tough enough to survive in an interdenominational milieu. The LCA has participated in theological discussions on an official level with both Presbyterians and Roman Catholics. The areas of agreement have been encouraging. However, the discussions also need to take place on the congregational level, involving key laymen in the parishes. Such opportunities need to be not only encouraged but promoted.

The Lutheran confessional position places her more com-patibly with Roman Catholicism than with Protestantism in gen-eral. This would seem to give her added responsibility for ecu-menical involvement. In fact it will be increasingly difficult for American Lutherans to maintain their biblical and confessional integrity apart from significant involvement with both Roman Catholics and Protestants. George Lindbeck argues for such involvement, observing that it is becoming increasingly difficult to develop a theological justification for either Protestantism or Roman Catholicism as they now exist. For the sake of the united

Christian witness which is our responsibility to the world and also for the sake of integrity in our theological work, we are compelled to strive for a church which is both Catholic and Reformed and lacks the doctrinal presumptuousness characteristic of existing denominations. Pelikan issues a similar challenge when he writes that Lutherans must find a way to be authentically confessional, simultaneously more Catholic and more Reformed than now. To settle for Lutheran unity, turning away from its Roman Catholic and its Protestant brethren, will lose both Catholic substance and Protestant principle. Lutheranism stands a chance of finding the new life and unity it needs, of reinterpreting both Catholic substance and Protestant principle, by taking part in the ecumenical enterprise.

# The Church and Its Mission

## I. THE CONTEXT: AN ERA OF
## RADICAL RE-EVALUATION

Radical re-evaluation of traditional concepts of the church and its mission appears to be the order of the day, together with attempts to create an ecclesiology consonant with the shape of contemporary society and with dominant motifs in contemporary theology. Currently there is a nearly exclusive emphasis on the function or mission of the church—an emphasis that is virtually a preoccupation. It contrasts starkly with the strong emphasis which earlier eras placed on the being or nature of the church. The current emphasis is manifested in diverse ways: the World Council of Churches' study of the structure of the missionary congregation, greater church involvement in current social issues, virulent criticisms of existing denominational and congregational structures, a vital interest in liturgical renewal.

Current emphasis is on the world or society as the arena for God's activity. The church shares in God's action and witnesses to it, according to this viewpoint, insofar as it participates in the world and society. "The world determines the agenda for the church." In previous periods the emphasis tended to be on the church as the locus of God's activity and on the church as God's witness to individuals and society. While the church was recognized as being in some sense in the world, it also was thought of as being qualitatively different from other human institutions because of its divine origin, nature, and purpose.

J. G. Davies, chairman of the western European study group for the World Council of Churches' study of the missionary structure of the congregation, provides a diagrammatic illustration of the difference between contemporary and more traditional views of the church. The traditional sequence of God→church→ world signified that God is primarily related to the church and related to the world only by means of the church. This view maintains that God relates himself to the world through the church in order to gather into the church as many persons from the world as possible.

Much current thought about the church uses a different sequence: God→world→church. This means that God's primary relation is to the world; the world, not the church, is the focus of God's plan. God is present in the world just as much as he is present in the church. The logic of such a position leaves little room for the church. Only when the church lets herself be used for God's dealings with the world is she true to her own nature. The center of attention is the world. The church exists to serve the world. The authenticity and effectiveness of that service are the criteria by which the church is judged.

In the ecclesiologies of previous generations, the church was regarded as the instrument or agent through which God speaks to the world. God entrusted the saving message of the gospel to the church, which proclaimed it to the world. Those outside the church had little hope of knowing God unless they accepted the message proclaimed by the church and entered its fellowship. Those in the church were called out of the world into the church. There was a tendency to regard the church as a colony of heaven, as the kingdom of God, at least in embryo. The church was the locus of all valid religious experience and activities. Although the church existed within the world, there were clear lines of demarcation which separated it from the world.

This type of ecclesiology led to certain consequences. The church was, ideally, a colony of heaven. If it was to be true to God's intention for it, those in it had to know with some theological precision what God intended its nature to be. Consequently, attention was focused on such ontological marks of the church as unity, holiness, catholicity, and apostolicity. The observable church was to be an embodiment of God's intention. Therefore the refinement and preservation of its organizational and institutional forms were of great importance. Its organizational extension in terms of geography and its numerical expansion in terms of numbers were requirements for the growth of God's kingdom. Since entry to the kingdom was effected by an individual's response to God's message proclaimed by the church, the church's proclamation aimed at the conversion of great numbers of individuals. For those who responded, life within the church comprised all religious experience and expression, encouraging a compartmentalization and privatization of religion.

Current thought about the church tends to select a somewhat different formulation of the relationship between church and world. Philip Hefner has clarified the rationale which seems to underlie the current consensus. It starts with the assumption that the church is not charged with the creation of a Christian society coextensive with the world. The church is simply one of many segments of society. It is distinguished from others by its desire to respond publicly to the call and action of God and to manifest that call and action by a Christian presence in society. The church seeks to discover and interpret how God is at work in the world and to participate in that work. The world, rather than the church, is regarded as the locus of God's activity. The church is to be a presence in society and to engage in dialogue rather than to be an autonomous institution that engages in proclamation.

The chief consequence of this viewpoint is an emphasis on the function or mission of the church. The church exists to serve the world, to forward God's activity in the world, to articulate and interpret his activity in dialogue with the world. The nature and the form of the church are of little importance. All that is required is that there be Christians, persons committed to God and to serving him in the world. Their association with one another as a people of God, a Christian koinonia, is for the sake of equipping themselves to serve the world. Such a position leads quite naturally to a disparagement of organizational and institutional forms of church life, particularly when concern about life within the forms distracts a Christian from what is regarded as his primary responsibility, serving the world. The world, not the church, becomes the center of religious experience and expression.

## Perspective: The Kingdom of God

To discuss the church's nature and mission is to describe its relationship to God and its relationship to the world. Such a discussion must also be concerned with the relationship between God and the world. The concept of the kingdom of God expressed in the Bible and developed by Christian theology is the broader background against which the relationships among God, world, and church need to be viewed.

The tapestry of tradition woven through the centuries by the Jewish people to portray the expected kingdom was rich in color and contrast. From the earliest days of their own self-conscious identity the Hebrews declared that God was their ruler and protector. In Judges 8:23 Gideon declined to be made king with the words: "I will not rule over you, and my son will not rule over you; the Lord will rule over you." In 1 Samuel 8:7 God tells Samuel that by asking Saul to be their ruler the Hebrews ". . . have not rejected you, but they have rejected me from being king over them."

Through the centuries the Hebrew concept of God was expanded until he was recognized as supreme over the entire world. "For God is the king of all the earth; . . . God reigns over the nations" (Psalm 47:7-8a). Two approaches to God's supremacy developed. The more popular one was that Israel held unique favor with God and that through Israel God would eventually assert his authority over all nations. "Behold, a day of the Lord is coming . . . I will gather all the nations against Jerusalem to battle . . . Then the Lord will go forth and fight against those nations . . . And the Lord will become king over

all the earth; on that day the Lord will be one and his name one"
(Zechariah 14:1-3, 9).

The other approach, presented in the deeper insights of the
prophets, was that God would use Israel as his means of revealing himself to all nations.

> He was despised and rejected by men;
>> a man of sorrows, and acquainted with grief;
> and as one from whom men hide their faces
>> he was despised, and we esteemed him not. . . .

> Yet it was the will of the Lord to bruise him;
>> he has put him to grief;
> when he makes himself an offering for sin,
>> he shall see his offspring, he shall prolong his days; . . .

> by his knowledge shall the righteous one, my servant,
>> make many to be accounted righteous;
>> and he shall bear their iniquities (Isaiah 53:3, 10-11).

Combined with this tradition in Israel's later days was rich
imagery that portrayed God with his angels and archangels and
all the hosts of good in battle with Satan and his demons and
all the forces of evil. Originally borrowed from the Persians, the
concept of the universe in the throes of a gigantic universal war
helped the Jews to explain why they and their Lord were meeting with defeat and foreign domination. The popular explanation
was that Satan was currently in control of the battle and of the
world. But the Day of Judgment would come when the righteous
would be raised from the dead, the forces of evil would be
defeated, and the rule of the Lord would be ushered in.

Evidently Jesus rejected the idea of a military kingdom with
Jerusalem as the center. At no point in his ministry is there even
a hint of the spirit of Ezekiel's valley filled with the bones of
the enemies of the kingdom. The passages in Isaiah 49, 52, and
53, which describe the suffering servant of God, are in keeping
with his spirit.

The theme of the kingdom is introduced at the beginning of Jesus' ministry, by his association with John the Baptist and John's message: "Repent, for the kingdom of heaven is at hand" (Matthew 3:2). The temptations he faced during the forty days in the wilderness revolved around ways he might fulfill his messianic role.

In Luke's Gospel Jesus comes from the wilderness of temptation to the synagogue in Nazareth. There he opens the scroll of Isaiah to the beginning of Chapter 61, and in an act that at least indicates the apostolic understanding of his mission and at most communicates his own conception of his task, he reads:

"The Spirit of the Lord is upon me,
because he has anointed me to preach good news to the poor.
He has sent me to proclaim release to the captives
and recovering of sight to the blind,
to set at liberty those who are oppressed,
to proclaim the acceptable year of the Lord."

And he closed the book and gave it back to the attendant, and sat down; and the eyes of all in the synagogue were fixed on him. And he began to say to them, "Today this scripture has been fulfilled in your hearing" (Luke 4:18-21).

How could the concept of Jesus' mission and the kingdom be plainer than in his reply to the disciples of John the Baptist? From prison John sent two of his followers to ask Jesus: "Are you he who is to come, or shall we look for another?" Jesus replies: "Go and tell John what you have seen and heard: the blind receive their sight, the lame walk, lepers are cleansed, and the deaf hear, the dead are raised up, the poor have good news preached to them. And blessed is he who takes no offense at me" (Luke 7:20, 22-23).

The gospel that Jesus proclaimed was that the kingdom of God was at hand. Already the signs of the rule of the Lord were being shown to those who accepted allegiance to him and followed his will. Here was a realm in which love was the guiding motivation and in which selfishness, cruelty, hostility, oppression, and exclusiveness had no place. It was obvious, then as now, that the majority of mankind had not begun to participate in the kingdom. But some had. And in them the kingdom was already at work in the world. When some Pharisees asked Jesus when the kingdom would come, he said: "The kingdom of God is not coming with signs to be observed; nor will they say, 'Lo, here it is!' or 'There!' for behold, the kingdom of God is in the midst of you" (Luke 17:20-21).

In this same passage Jesus goes on to describe the coming of the Son of man in a dramatic, universe-shaking manner also. In the teachings of Christ a balance is developed between viewing the kingdom as a present phenomenon, growing as quietly and rapidly as a mustard seed, and the kingdom as being ushered in dramatically by a Day of Judgment and Wrath in which those who did not feed the hungry and clothe the naked will have the door to relationship with God slammed in their faces. No matter which manifestation Jesus is describing, however, he makes completely clear the point that the kingdom is not the possession of any one person or any group of people. The kingdom belongs to God, and its outreach is to the world.

In Christ's great prayer he says, "As thou didst send me into the world, so I have sent them into the world" (John 17:18). The Great Commission (Matthew 28:19-20) clearly states the early church's understanding of its task as being consistent with the "little gospel" in John: "For God so loved the world that he gave his only Son, that whoever believes in him should not perish but have eternal life. For God sent the Son into the world, not to condemn the world, but that the world might be saved through him" (John 3:16-17).

Membership in the kingdom was not to be understood as a status symbol. The call to accept the reign, instead, was a summons to let the will of God permeate the earth as salt permeates meat. Jesus directed the members of the kingdom to become the leaven and light of society. This figure of speech makes obsolutely no sense if the kingdom involves man's withdrawal from the social, political, economic, and technological issues of the day. The idea of God gathering his followers around him for a ghetto-like existence negates the picture of the kingdom presented in the New Testament.

Now, to summarize, the biblical-theological concept of the kingdom of God has important implications for the relationships among God, world, and church. The kingdom of God is God's rule, with an emphasis on functional relationships rather than spatial models. It is brought about by God's action and man's response to that action. God's kingdom introduces a new age which has already begun in Christ but which is not yet perfectly fulfilled. The kingdom of God is his rule over all creation and acknowledgment of his sovereignty by all creation. Redemption effected by Christ frees man for entrance into the kingdom. God's kingdom will come to fulfillment when all mankind acknowledges and lives under his sovereignty, either in history or beyond history.

In the interim, individuals who accept the relationship with God which Christ established enter the kingdom. They become part of a community of believers, a community charged with the responsibility of living in such a manner that others may enter the kingdom. All who enter live henceforth in both the kingdom (insofar as they live under God's rule) and in the world which does not acknowledge God's rule. The church is the community of believers. But it is not the kingdom of God; it is part of the kingdom in that it exists within the total creation which is the scope of the kingdom. It exists for the sake of the kingdom and looks and works toward its ultimate realization, acting as God's agent in history.

## II. THE BEING (NATURE) OF THE CHURCH

For purposes of analysis it is helpful to separate the question of the being or nature of the church from the question of its function or mission. Even so, the analysis must never lose sight of the organic relationship between being and function. What is set forth as normative for the nature of the church must facilitate the performance of its mission. Any description of the church's mission must be consistent with its nature.

Descriptions of the nature of the church serve two purposes. By identifying normative characteristics of the church, they provide goals to be sought in the life of the church; they also provide a way of determining when and where the church exists. The classical Reformation documents describe three marks which are considered to indicate the existence of the true church. They are (1) the visible congregation of saints in which (2) the gospel is rightly taught, and (3) the sacraments are rightly administered. Other creedal and confessional statements describe characteristics felt to be basic to the church's existence: unity, holiness, catholicity, and apostolicity.

An increasing number of Protestant theologians are questioning the adequacy of the traditional Protestant descriptions of the church. Too often the descriptions have been interpreted in a static manner, with major emphasis being placed upon geographical and institutional concerns. It has been pointed out that, within the framework of these descriptions, the church has often developed an attitude similar to that which Jesus rejected in the Judaism dominant in his day. The messianic hope in that era tended to be a looking forward to the coming of a Messiah as an event which would establish Israel in its glory at the center of the nations of the world. A dominant trend in Christianity has been to look back to the first Advent which called all men into the organized church, and to look forward to the second Advent as the event which is to make the call unambiguously clear. In this context the church's mission has often been regarded as recruitment of members rather than as the role of a servant of God whose role is to witness to his kingdom.

Biblical figures of speech describing the church help to clarify the nature of the church and its mission, and the organic relationship of the two. The biblical images highlight the nature of the church as a people of God, consisting of persons who live in fellowship with him and with one another. The church as the people of God comes into existence as persons respond to God's action in Christ. It accepts the role of a servant whose responsibility is to serve God and witness to him in the world.

The most familiar biblical image is Paul's concept of the church as the body of Christ: "So we, though many, are one body in Christ, and individually members one of another" (Romans 12:5). "He is the head of the body, the church; . . ." (Colossians 1:18). Another term designates the church as the bride that is loved by Christ, the husband: "Come, I will show you the Bride, the wife of the Lamb" (Revelation 21:9). A third figure portrays the church as a building of which Christ is the cornerstone: "So then you are no longer strangers and sojourners, but you are fellow citizens with the saints and members of the household of God, built upon the foundations of the apostles and prophets, Christ Jesus himself being the cornerstone, in whom the whole structure is joined together and grows into a holy temple in the Lord" (Ephesians 2:19-21).

A contemporary description of the church closely related to the biblical idea of the body of Christ is that the church is an extension of the Incarnation. This concept has been criticized and amended by T. W. Manson, who prefers to think of the life of the church as the continuation of the messianic ministry of Christ. The biblical and the contemporary images of the church emphasize the integral relationship between the church and Jesus Christ and his messianic role. As Messiah he inaugurated the kingdom of God. The role of the church is to live within and to testify to the kingdom.

A tension exists between prescriptive and descriptive discussions of the nature of the church. Prescriptive definitions start with biblical images; descriptive definitions are unable to identify any empirical or observable characteristics which correspond to the biblical-theological images. Prescriptive definitions emphasize such characteristics as unity, holiness, catholicity, apostolicity; descriptive definitions find evidence that these characteristics do not exist (unless they are interpreted in terms not susceptible to empirical verification). The tension between the prescriptive and the descriptive is resolved by the Reformation definition of the church as the congregation of saints in which the gospel is rightly preached and the sacraments rightly administered.

## III. THE FUNCTION (MISSION) OF THE CHURCH

Current thinking about the church is almost exclusively thinking about its mission. Werner Elert wrote that the church can exist only to the extent that it *is* the mission. J. C. Hoekendijk wrote that the nature of the church can be adequately defined by its function of participation in Christ's ministry. The emphasis on mission is a reaction to the earlier emphasis on the church's nature, which was accompanied by an emphasis on institutionalized religion. The point is made most vividly by those who maintain that the church exists only as God's mission is fulfilled, that the church has no identity or existence apart from that mission. The church is regarded as a sign in the world—a sign which

More than a few leaders feel that the church has run counter points toward and is used for the kingdom.

to its commission. Instead of sending people into the world, it has too often acted as if it were a haven into which people might escape from the world. Instead of demonstrating that God's salvation pertains to those people who are in the grime of life, it has too frequently acted as if salvation were a prized possession of those who have withdrawn from soiling contact with life. Instead of recognizing that its role is to witness to the kingdom, it has acted as if it were to institutionalize the kingdom.

One of the clearest New Testament statements about the church is 1 Peter 2:9: "But you are a chosen race, a royal priesthood, a holy nation, God's own people, that you may declare the wonderful deeds of him who has called you out of darkness into his marvelous light." The church has often assumed that in order to fulfill this vocation, God's people must exist as the gathered community concerned primarily about their own spiritual needs and about bringing others into the community. The text does not justify such an assumption. The meaning of the text is that the church is a community of servants called and committed to go out into the world as the bearers of the good news of what God has done for all. This understanding is faithful to the biblical understanding of the universal dimensions of God's redemptive action. Christ has changed the human situation. New possibilities of life have been opened for all. The church is the sign of the new humanity. God also gathers his people; yet when the gathering creates the type of church which is not free to fulfill the task for which it was called into existence, something is wrong.

When the church is a community of servants or witnesses, a type of spirituality may develop which will attract those most concerned about participating in Christ's work in our modern world. A form of institutional life may develop which will make it possible to overcome ecclesiastical self-centeredness. Lutherans stand in a preferred position to do something about the calls that come repeatedly from contemporary thinkers for new forms of church life that will assist in fulfilling the function of the church in the twentieth century. Because they have traditionally regarded polity and structure as *adiaphora*, they have been free to adopt a greater variety of organization than any other Christian denomination. This freedom now needs to be extended beyond a freedom to choose between old forms into a freedom to experiment with new forms. Even though structure does not stand at the heart of the gospel, it is not unimportant. It has made itself important by becoming a hindrance to the kerygma. The church, which should have been present in the world in the posture of a loving servant, has too frequently given the appearance of a prince or president, or at least a well-fed member of the middle class.

Luther recognized the tension between viewing the church as an institution and viewing it as God's servant in the world. He said that when "Christian" comes to the altar in church he finds to his surprise that Christ has his hand up. "I don't need your gift," Christ says, "but your neighbor does." So he sends "Christian" back out into the world to his neighbor, a process that is upsetting to "Christian" because Christ has sent him away. But then "Christian" finds that when he gets out to his neighbor, Christ is there, saying, "Now I will receive your gift." The real church, Luther pointed out, takes shape around the way in which we are driven by Christ to find him in the act of obedience. The church takes shape in the way in which we serve the neighbor's need in the world.

The initial Assembly of the East India Christian Conference in 1959 stated: "Each congregation must know that it is put into the world by the Lord as His representative, and that it must therefore be chiefly concerned, not with itself, but with the world; concerned to send its members out as witnesses, and to invite all men into the family of God. Its minister should be one who is seeking to train every member for this ministry in the world. . . . Its forms of organization should be such that every member can be, and know himself to be, an active member in the Body of Christ." (*Concept III*, World Council of Churches Department on Studies in Evangelism, Geneva, January 1963).

The report of Section I of the Fourth World Conference on Faith and Order held in Montreal raised critical questions:

—If the church is the body of the crucified Lord, can it expect more honor than he received?

—If the glory and victory of the Lord is his exaltation on the cross, can the church attain a greater glory than by following gladly, even into suffering at the hands of men?

—If the church professes to follow the Lord who spent his time with publicans and sinners, why does it look so much like a congregation of scribes and pharisees?

—If the Lord of the church was crucified outside the city, why is the church so comfortable within its walls and so hesitant to risk bearing its witness in efforts to establish justice and mercy?

—If Christ was flesh and blood and if he is the Lord of all creation, how can his followers so often flee into a spirituality that divorces God from earth and its possibilities?

Increasingly it is recognized that Christians must not be content with charitable activities but must help unions, must be active in employers councils and housing committees, must work for racial integration, must campaign for aid to Americans who live in poverty, and must make the cause of depressed peoples everywhere a matter of conscience. We must be reminded constantly that Christ died not only or even primarily for the church, but for the world.

The function or mission of the church is to serve as one means by which the world may come more perfectly under the rule of God. It serves by articulating and interpreting God's revelation of himself as it occurs in the world, by engaging in dialogue with the world, not by attempting to impose its view on the world. It serves as a channel for God's redemptive activity by witnessing to the gospel. The church should constantly be aware of the extent to which it embodies God's presence in the world and the extent of its failure to do so.

The recent World Council of Churches study document on the biblical concept of conversion stresses both the Christian's relationship to God and his consequent relationship to the world. The concept of the kingdom of God is seen as essential to the biblical understanding of conversion. The fallacy of regarding personal commitment as an end in itself is pointed out as stress is put on the indivisibility of the whole man and the total society, personal and social justice, individuals and social structures. Those who are called to be Christian are called for the sake of the world. Even though conversion and baptism are linked with entrance into the church in a historical sense, they serve the larger purpose of God for all of creation rather than the purpose of the church.

The tension between prescriptive and descriptive definitions exists with regard to the mission of the church as well as with regard to its nature. The prescriptive definition of the church's mission as the servant of God in the world implies that the attention of the church should be focused on God and on the world, that there should be a minimum of self-consciousness and self-concern on the part of the church. When descriptions of the empirical church are set alongside this norm, the deficiencies are marked.

George W. Webber observes that in nineteenth-century America the mainstream of Christian tradition affirmed that the kingdom of God was within the individual. It believed that men, living in the power of God, were the agents of God's activity in the world. This was the self-determined Puritan Protestant, a rugged individualist confident that God blessed those who worked hard and who were God-fearing. The result was an individualistic moralism unable to face the problems of the emerging world of industrialism and mass society.

Then a shift took place. In response to the needs of modern society, the church sought to express the kingdom of God through institutions and a variety of voluntary organizations. The church as an institution became the locus of the kingdom of God. Church work came to mean what is done within the gathered life of the church. The church became cut off from the world of politics and economics, irrelevant to the struggle of men and nations for meaning and for true humanity. The church became a human institution, judged by human standards. There was no tension between the church and the world because a secularized Christian church was cheerfully accepted by a pseudo-Christian society.

There is a strong tradition that interprets the aim of evangelism as the planting or extension of the church. Missions are seen as the road from the church to the church. It is the outgoing activity of one church to a location where a new church is planted. In principle, the task of missions is completed as soon as this church exists. It is possible to justify this position. But it involves a temptation to take the church itself too seriously, to invite the church to see itself as God's secure bridgehead in the world, to think of itself as having what others do not have and distributing its possessions to others until a new group of Christians is formed.

Such a position is not unknown in American Lutheranism. Until a few years before its merger into the Lutheran Church in America, the United Lutheran Church of America sponsored a publication called *Ecclesia Plantanda*. The thought that the organized church must be planted had wide acceptance among people who regarded the church as being in a mediating relationship between God and world. The extension of the church as an institution was the most natural means for extending the realm of redemption, for it was within the church that God ruled. *Ecclesia Plantanda* was published by the Board of American Missions of the ULCA. Such thinking as it implied, however, has not been foreign to world missions' interests.

Ironically, some Roman Catholic missiologists have moved into the position being vacated by the Protestants. Within the last two decades they have accepted church extension and mission as being somewhat synonymous, and they have felt that doing so was a healthy action about which they could be enthusiastic. Dr. Ronan Hoffman, Professor of Missiology at the Catholic University of America, pointed to the shift in Roman Catholic thinking in a paper he delivered in 1964 to the academic organization of Protestant professors of missions. He cited the work of the Belgian Jesuit missiologist Pierre Charles, who concluded in 1938 that the specific objective of the mission apostolate was the establishment of the visible church in the regions where it did not yet exist. The concept of *implantatio ecclesiae* led to a revolution in Catholic missionary thinking. The dominant purpose of missions had been expressed for centuries in terms of preaching the gospel and propagating the Christian faith among non-Christians, aimed at the conversion and salvation of their souls.

Dr. Hoffman felt that the "Charles theory" had made a contribution, since it had brought awareness of the global responsibility of the predominantly Western church into the mainstream of Roman Catholic thinking. Without this step the Roman Catholic church would not now be ready to examine the apostolate in greater depth. The "Charles theory" was important because it brought together for the first time in Catholic circles the ideas of "church" and "mission." It led to an understanding of their intimate relationship. Catholic thinkers have come to recognize the necessity for conceiving of missionary action in terms of the church, to realize the essentially missionary character of the church.

Further development of Roman Catholic thought about the nature of the church is evidenced by the fifth general chapter of the Maryknoll Fathers in the fall of 1966. Lasting from August 1 to October 26, it was the longest chapter in the history of the Catholic Foreign Mission Society (official title of the Maryknoll group). The society's leadership re-examined the apostolate and the purpose, function, and characteristics of Maryknoll in the light of developments at Vatican II. Although the resulting document keeps the organized church in center stage, it indicates that the princely church is deliberately beginning to take off its expensive robes in order to become the serving church.

The report states that long-standing priorities in mission policy must be examined in the light of the church's own understanding of herself as sign or sacrament of salvation. The ultimate criterion of a valid missionary enterprise is the amount of time, energy, and resources which the Christian community devotes to Christian witness, that is, to the genuine love and service of their fellow men. When this criterion is not present, the sign of salvation is lacking, the core of missionary activity is lacking, the church is not authentically present. The total structure of a missionary program should grow organically out of the requirements of Christian witness. Thus it is a mistake to look upon any or all of the following as valid criteria of the success of missionary efforts in isolation from the demands of Christian witness: pastoral statistics (numbers of converts, catechumens, communions, infant baptism); attendance at Mass and parish devotions; mission personnel statistics (such as numbers of clergy and religious engaged in mission work); parish activities, societies, and institutions with numerous active members; buildings to accommodate diocesan and parochial activities, with ample real estate holdings to provide for future expansion; financial solvency; the attainment of a high degree of respectability and influence in social and political life; amicable relationships between clergy, religious, and laity in the conduct of parish life. These may well be characteristics of a truly vital, witnessing community. But they could also apply to a situation where Christians are self-centered and unconcerned with presenting the sign of salvation to the world through their service of their fellow men. Some of them may even hinder the church's role as sign and her effective presence in the community.

Some Protestants have been so vigorous in their attack on a self-centered church that they have sounded as if the organized church should be discarded. Others feel that the organized church has lost itself in irrelevancies, but instead of disbanding it, they would call it from concentration on expanding itself to concentration on expanding itself in fulfilling its mission in the world. Perhaps a tension between the church as an organization and the church as a servant of God in the world always will and always should exist. On the one hand, a degree of organization is required for the performance of mission. On the other hand, the organization must be prohibited from assuming any value beyond its usefulness in realizing the purposes of God in relation to the world.

The Lutheran Church in America's work in Japan will serve as an example of the tension between mission and institution. There the LCA ideally assumes the form of a loving servant in relation to the Japanese people. It places its resources and its organization at the disposal of the mission. The mission requires them, yet they must never assume any inherent importance. One phase of proclaiming the realm of redemption in Japan is to call Japanese to accept Jesus as savior and God as lord. Those who respond then require an organized church through which they, in turn, can fulfill the mission.

At this point, however, confusion sometimes develops. Some Americans and some Japanese mistakenly assume that the Japanese are called to serve the church which Lutherans from America have planted. They fail to recognize that the church there is called into being to serve the Japanese as they participate in the kingdom. Especially in such a situation as in Japan, the implicit dangers of church organization can be seen. Believing that they were serving God, western Christians imported a religious structure so overwhelming in its complexity that Japanese Christians become exhausted before they can turn their attention to fulfilling the apostolate within the world. In the Kyodan, for example, 70 percent of the congregations have less than 100 members, yet each congregation consistently attempts to support a full-time seminary-trained pastor whose primary task, in turn, becomes that of serving the organized church. The person who wishes to engage in mission frequently must escape.

Much of this discussion about the church in Japan also applies to the church in Canada and the United States. As long as we view a situation from a distance, we can analyze it much more objectively; so Japan is used as a mirror. Viewing the tension between the church as an institution and the church as mission realistically is not something for Lutherans in America to fear. They have honored precedent for doing so in Luther's appraisals of institutionalized religion.

Prophetic voices within the church have pointed to the increasing irrelevance of Protestantism to the central issues of modern life, notes George W. Webber. "A secularized church in a pseudo-Christian culture" deals chiefly with the private, personal world and is largely peripheral to the public realm. In Europe the problem for the church is more clear-cut; men have simply stopped bothering with the churches.

In America the religious interest has led to the extensive "churchification" of suburbia and has given the impression of Christian vitality and widespread commitment to the church. Only gradually has it become apparent that the suburban boom may mask a withdrawal of Christian responsibility for the mission of the church. There are signs of great restlessness as men and women ask what their busyness is all about, whether it is in fact God's work that is demanding their energy and devotion. Some observers have gone so far as to say that God has been forced to go outside the organized church to find those who will accomplish his mission. The church has not only become irrelevant to man, it has in a sense become irrelevant to God also.

Tension between prescriptive and descriptive definitions of the church in mission can be resolved, in theory, by a withering away of ecclesiastical organization. This may occur if there is a continuation and growth of an unorganized "underground church," of "detached" or "anonymous" Christians, of informal cell groups even within congregations. The church has continued to exist in such forms in contemporary times in countries where Christians have been subjected to harassment and persecution.

It is questionable whether such a withering away of church structure will occur in areas where Christians do not encounter strong overt opposition. The existence of church structure provides avenues of service to the world which might have to be invented if they did not already exist. In a thoughtful article about the question of church growth, David Stowe points out the values inherent in church structures and numerical growth if they are always regarded as means to the end of mission and never are allowed to become ends in themselves. In many respects they have become ends in themselves for the life of North American churches in the mid-twentieth century. There is need for a radical re-orientation of dominant viewpoints regarding the institutional church and a transformation of the organization. There must be a balanced emphasis on nature and mission. There must be a greater willingness to engage in risk-taking experimentation. There must be a renewed sense of being God's servants in and to the world.

In the early 1930's Tillich predicted that the church would cease to function in modern secular society unless it could repossess the sacred by clothing it in symbolic and sacramental forms that communicate to contemporary man, unless it could demonstrate the intrinsic unity of the sacred and the secular, and unless it could maintain prophetic insight and power in pronouncing judgment on the claims for absolute authority made by secular institutions. These three tasks can be regarded as contemporary requirements for making known the meaning of the kingdom of God. Their fulfillment may well come by means of ecclesiastical organizations, but only by means of ecclesiastical organizations which regard themselves as servants of God in the world and for the world.

# Selected Bibliography

*Chapter One. Theological Responses to the Present Challenge.*

Braaten, Carl E. *New Directions in Theology Today: History and Hermeneutics*, Volume II. Philadelphia: Westminster Press, 1966.

Cobb, John B. *A Christian Natural Theology.* Philadelphia: Westminster Press, 1965.

Cobb, John B. "Christian Natural Theology and Christian Existence," *The Christian Century* (March 3, 1965).

Cobb, John B. "A New Trio Arises in Europe," *Christian Advocate* (July 2, 1964). Reprinted in *New Theology No. 2*, ed. Martin E. Marty and Dean G. Peerman. New York: Macmillan, 1965.

Curtis, C. J. "The Living God Theology," *The Ecumenist*, V (November-December, 1966).

Hordern, William. *New Directions in Theology Today, Introduction*, Volume I. Philadelphia: Westminster Press, 1966.

Lazareth, William H. "The Future of American Lutheranism," *Protestant Churches and Reform Today*, ed. William Wolff. New York: Seabury Press, 1964.

Lilje, Hanns. *Luther Now.* Philadelphia: Muhlenberg Press, 1946.

MacQuarrie, John. *New Directions in Theology Today: God and Secularity*, Volume III. Philadelphia: Westminster Press, 1967.

MacQuarrie, John. *Studies in Christian Existentialism.* Philadelphia: Westminster Press, 1966.

Ogden, Schubert. *The Reality of God.* New York: Harper and Row, 1966.

Pannenberg, Wolfhart. "The Crisis of the Scripture-Principle in Protestant Theology," *Dialog*, II (Fall, 1963).

Pannenberg, Wolfhart. "Did Jesus Really Rise from the Dead?" *Dialog*, IV (Spring, 1965).

Pannenberg, Wolfhart. "Review of Tillich's *Systematic Theology*," *Dialog*, IV (Summer, 1965).

Robinson, James M. and John B. Cobb (eds.). *New Frontiers in Theology; The Later Heidegger and Theology*, Volume I. New York: Harper and Row, 1963.

Robinson, James M. and John B. Cobb (eds.). *New Frontiers in Theology: Theology as History*, Volume III. New York: Harper and Row, 1967.

Teilhard de Chardin, Pierre. *The Phenomenon of Man*. New York: Harper and Row, 1959.

Tillich, Paul. *The Future of Religions*. New York: Harper and Row, 1966.

Williams, Daniel D. *What Present-Day Theologians Are Thinking*. Third edition. New York: Harper and Row, 1967.

*Chapter Two. Biblical Interpretation*

Bartsch, H. W. (ed.). *Kerygma and Myth*. New York: Harper and Row, 1961.

Bornkamm, Gunther. *Jesus of Nazareth*. New York: Harper and Row, 1960.

Burke, T. P. (ed.). *The Word in History*. New York: Sheed and Ward, 1966.

Ebeling, Gerhard. *Theology and Proclamation*. Philadelphia: Fortress Press, 1966.

Flender, Helmut. *St. Luke: Theologian of Redemptive History*. Philadelphia: Fortress Press, 1967.

Fuller, Reginald H. *The New Testament in Current Study*. New York: Scribner, 1962.

Funk, Robert W. *Language, Hermeneutic, and Word of God*. New York: Harper and Row, 1966.

Pannenberg, Wolfhart. *Jesus—God and Man*. Philadelphia: Westminster Press, 1968.

Reumann, John and William Lazareth. *Righteousness and Society*. Philadelphia: Fortress Press, 1967. (See Ch. 1, "The New Testament—Documents from a Revolutionary Age in the Revolution of Modern Study.")

Robinson, James M. *A New Quest of the Historical Jesus*. Naperville, Ill.: Allenson, 1959.

Robinson, James M. and John B. Cobb (eds.). *New Frontiers in Theology Today: The New Hermeneutic*, Volume II. New York: Harper and Row, 1964.

Stendahl, Krister. "Biblical Theology, Contemporary," *The Interpreter's Dictionary of the Bible*, I. New York: Abingdon Press, 1962. pp. 418-32.

Von Rad, Gerhard. *Old Testament Theology*, 2 vols. New York: Harper and Row, 1966.

Westermann, Claus (ed.). *Essays on Old Testament Hermeneutics*. Richmond, Va.: John Knox Press, 1963.

Zahrnt, Heinz. *The Historical Jesus*. New York: Harper and Row, 1963.

*Chapter Three. Christian Ethics*

Bennett, John C. (ed.). *Christian Social Ethics in a Changing World*. New York: Association Press, 1966.

Cox, Harvey. *The Secular City*. New York: Macmillan, 1965.

Elert, Werner. *The Christian Ethos*. Philadelphia: Fortress Press, 1957.

Gustafson, James M. "Context versus Principles: A Misplaced Debate in Christian Ethics," *Harvard Theological Review* (April, 1965). Reprinted in *New Theology No. 3*, ed. Martin E. Marty and Dean G. Peerman. New York: Macmillan, 1966.

Hefner, Philip. "Therapeutic Man: Post-Christian and Post-Community," *Una Sancta*, XXIII, Michael and All Angels, 1966.

Lehmann, Paul. *Ethics in a Christian Context*. New York: Harper and Row, 1963.

Mooney, Christopher F. "Risk in Teilhard de Chardin," *Christianity and Crisis* (April 8, 1965).

Novak, Michael. "Secular Style and Natural Law," *Christianity and Crisis* (July 26, 1965).

Ramsey, Paul. *Deeds and Rules in Christian Ethics*. New York: Scribner, 1967.

Rogers, William B. "Personality and the Ethical Dynamism," *The Christian Scholar*, XL (Winter, 1962).

Sittler, Joseph. *The Structure of Christian Ethics*. Baton Rouge, La.: Louisiana State University Press, 1958.

Thielicke, Helmut. *Theological Ethics: Foundations*, Volume I. Philadelphia: Fortress Press, 1966.

Tillich, Paul. *Love, Power, and Justice*. New York: Oxford University Press, 1960.

Walther, Christian. "The Problem of Theology and Society," *Faith and Society*, Supplement to *Lutheran World*, No. 2, 1966.

Winter, Gibson. *Elements for a Social Ethic*. New York: Macmillan, 1966.

## Chapter Four. Ecumenism, History, and Tradition

Baum, Gregory. *Progress and Perspectives: The Catholic Quest for Christian Unity*. New York: Sheed and Ward, 1962.

Bridston, Keith and W. D. Wagoner. *Unity in Mid-Career*. New York: Macmillan, 1962.

Brown, Edgar S., Jr. "The Worship of the Church and Modern Man," *Studia Liturgica* (March, 1963). Reprinted in *New Theology No. 1*, ed. Martin E. Marty and Dean G. Peerman. New York: Macmillan, 1964.

Cavert, Samuel M. *On the Road to Christian Unity*. New York: Harper and Row, 1961.

Lindbeck, George A. "Jewish-Christian Dialogue—I," *Journal of Ecumenical Studies*, III (Winter, 1966).

Mackay, John A. *Ecumenics—The Science of the Church Universal*. Englewood Cliffs, N. J.: Prentice-Hall, 1964.

Maurer, Wilhelm. "Dogma, History of," *Encyclopedia of the Lutheran Church*, I, ed. J. Bodensieck, Philadelphia: Fortress Press, 1965. pp. 720-34.

Minear, Paul S. (ed.). *The Nature of the Unity We Seek: Official Report of the North American Conference on Faith and Order.* St. Louis: Bethany Press, 1963.

Pauck, Wilhelm. *The Heritage of the Reformation.* New York: Free Press, 1961.

Pelikan, Jaroslav. "American Lutheranism: Denomination or Confession?" *What's Ahead for the Churches,* eds. Kyle Haselden and Martin E. Marty. New York: Sheed and Ward, 1964.

Pelikan, Jaroslav. *Obedient Rebels.* New York: Harper and Row, 1964.

Pelikan, Jaroslav. "Tradition, Reformation, and Development," *The Christian Century* (June 6, 1965).

Quanbeck, Warren A. "Confessional Integrity and Ecumenical Dialogue," *A Re-examination of Lutheran and Reformed Traditions—IV. Ethics and Ethos—Summaries and Comment.* New York: North American Area of the World Alliance of Reformed Churches and U.S.A. National Committee of the Lutheran World Federation, 1966.

Ramsey, A. M. "Unity, Holiness, and Truth," *Ecumenical Review,* XIV (January, 1962).

Shands, Alfred. *The Liturgical Movement and the Local Church.* New York: Morehouse-Barlow, 1965.

Skydsgaard, K. E. *One in Christ.* Philadelphia: Fortress Press, 1957.

Skydsgaard, K. E. "Why Lutherans Must Talk with Rome," *Dialog,* I (Summer, 1962).

Thurian, Max. *Visible Unity and Tradition.* Baltimore: Helicon Press, 1962.

## Chapter Five. The Church and Its Mission

Gensichen, Hans Werner. *Living Mission. The Test of Faith.* Philadelphia: Fortress Press, 1966.

Gustafson, James M. *Treasure in Earthen Vessels. The Church as a Human Community.* New York: Harper and Row, 1961.

Hefner, Philip. "Theological Reflections (2)" *Una Sancta*, XXIV, No. 4, Christmass, 1967.

Hoekendijk, J. C. *The Church Inside Out*. Philadelphia: Westminster Press, 1966.

Jenkins, Daniel. *The Strangeness of the Church*. New York: Doubleday, 1955.

Manson, T. W. *The Church's Ministry*. Philadelphia: Westminster Press, 1948.

Niebuhr, H. Richard. *Christ and Culture*. New York: Harper and Row, 1956.

Nygren, Anders (ed.). *This Is the Church*. Philadelphia: Muhlenberg Press, 1952.

Pannenberg, Wolfhart. "The Kingdom of God and the Church," *Una Sancta*, XXIV, No. 4, Christmass, 1967.

Rahner, Karl. *The Church after the Council*. New York: Herder and Herder. 1966.

Stowe, David M. "A Perspective on the Church Growth Question," *Information Service* (NCCCUSA), February 24, 1968.

Webber, George W. *The Congregation in Mission*. New York: Abingdon Press, 1964.

Wieser, Thomas (ed.). *Planning for Mission*. New York: U. S. Conference for the World Council of Churches, 1966.

Welch, Claude. *The Reality of the Church*. New York: Scribner, 1958.

World Council of Churches. *The Church for Others and the Church for the World. A Quest for Structures for Missionary Congregations. Final Report of the Western European Working Group and the North American Working Group of the Department on Studies in Evangelism*. Geneva: World Council of Churches, 1967.

World Council of Churches. *Conversion to God and Service to Man. A Study Document on the Biblical Concept of Conversion*. Geneva: World Council of Churches, 1967.